"Her supreme achievement is in the appealing humanity and fallibility of her characters." —THE NEW YORK TIMES

Also by

SIGRID UNDSET

Winner of the Nobel Prize for Literature *in* 1928

MODERN NOVELS

Jenny

The Winding Road
which comprises
The Wild Orchid and
The Burning Bush

Ida Elisabeth

The Longest Years

The Faithful Wife

Images in a Mirror

MEDIÆVAL ROMANCES

Kristin Lavransdatter

A TRILOGY

The Bridal Wreath
The Mistress of Husaby
The Cross

The Master of Hestviken

A TETRALOGY

The Axe
The Snake Pit
In the Wilderness
The Son Avenger

Gunnar's Daughter

ESSAYS

Stages on the Road

These are BORZOI BOOKS, *published by*
ALFRED A. KNOPF

MEN, WOMEN, AND PLACES

MEN, WOMEN, AND PLACES

BY

SIGRID UNDSET

Translated from the Norwegian by

ARTHUR G. CHATER

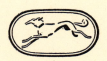

ALFRED A. KNOPF · NEW YORK
1939

CONTENTS

BLASPHEMY

 ON March 7, 1934 the Norwegian papers announced that the Storting had adopted an amendment of the " Blasphemy Clause," increasing its severity. It now reads as follows: " A person who publicly ridicules or scoffs at any confession of faith the practice of which is permitted in this Kingdom shall be punished by fine, arrest, or imprisonment " — and so on.

The direct cause of this amendment of the Blasphemy Clause was doubtless a much talked-of address by Arnulf Överland on scandalizing. And its aim can go no further than preventing — if possible — religious discussions and conflicts between the spokesmen of incompatible views of life from exceeding a certain limit of verbal propriety. In existing circumstances — here in Norway at the present time — it is obvious that law and authority cannot intervene in any other way. A State which asserts religious tolerance as a principle — which declares, in other words, that it respects men's right to disagree fundamentally on the questions of why we exist here on earth and what we intend to live and work and fight for — can go no further than attempting to prescribe what polemical methods are permissible and what is to be regarded as fair and decorous opposition. And if the amended Blasphemy Clause with its threats of penalties and so forth can lead to a more or less objective attitude in the battle of convictions, instead of letting it degenerate into sheer abuse and paroxysms of rage, that in itself will be no small gain. In any case those who consider it a concern of society as well as of the State to do what is possible to prevent an outbreak of the barbarous instincts latent in all of us cannot fail to welcome a law which has for its object the checking of the barbarians' propensity to rabid frenzy and psychopathic indulgence in gross vituperation, even in a conflict of opinions and beliefs.

On the other hand it is impossible to imagine any tribunal capable of determining whether a given religious system is in itself intrinsically blasphemous — whether its doctrine of the nature and works of God and its precepts regarding the nature and works of man constitute blasphemy. Even for that section of the nation which professes Christianity no such tribunal can be indicated. Within the State Church, as we all know, there is room for so many so-called " personal conceptions " of God that one section of its members must inevitably hold another group's subjective ideas of the nature of God to be presumptuous and blasphemous. I need only mention Professor Hallesby's *Christian Doctrine of Morals,*

4

which he has constructed on the basis of his *Christian Doctrine of Faith*. Both doctrines are bound up with a particular mentality — that of the professor himself — and with a particular milieu — the little congregations of religiously inclined families in the small towns and country districts of our sparsely populated land. These groups — they often chose to call themselves " Friends " or " Brethren " or something of the sort — necessarily included people of fairly homogeneous experience and a similar, sound, but not very far-reaching education; they were inclined to foster this homogeneity by evolving their own group language, by modelling their lives on certain types, not only in outward forms but in their intellectual development; and they regarded with the most profound distrust everything that was foreign to them and that they could not immediately understand on the basis of their own experience. As these Christian sects in their day — the last century — were in violent opposition to the clergy, who were drawn from another class, that of officialdom, and as this class, too, had its own Christian traditions, which in a way and with contributions from many new intellectual sources still persist, it is only natural that within the ranks of the same State Church one should meet with people whose conceptions of the God whom Jesus Christ called His Father are more irreconcilable than, for instance, the ideas of Romans and Egyptians about deities who differed in name and legend.

And they all appeal to the Bible. Only they read it in

such a way as to derive essentially different religions from it, since each one contributes something of his own. For it is not humanly possible for a man to read a book in such a way as to remember what he has read for three whole days without adding to it something of himself. One man combines his reading of the Bible with recollections of what he has read elsewhere, another with memories of his own experience. All his efforts to arrive at the true faith and the right doctrine have not sufficed to prevent Professor Hallesby from doing the same. When he tries to extract from the Bible what knowledge we can obtain from the words of Scripture about eternal life — the state of bliss — he arrives inevitably at the conclusion that we may permit ourselves the hope of finding hereafter all that our hearts cling to in this life, but in a transfigured state, so that our hearts may continue to cling to these things without any risk of their tempting us to sin. But: " Thus we shall find it all again on the resurrection morn: our beautiful country to which God has bound us by so many subtle ties; the dear surroundings of our home, with all their memories, which make an old spirit young again and a hard heart soft as wax; the old house in the golden gleam of childhood's memories; the horse, the dog, the cow, the cat, the sheep — we shall meet them all again! "

Professor Hallesby himself adds, however, that he does not *know* what the mountain or the horse or the dog will look like in a transfigured state. So that in his case, unlike that of others who assure me that we shall have domestic animals in eternity, one is less tempted to ask: What about the other animals? Will the tigers be so transfigured that they won't really be tigers any more? And if there is to be a fauna in the world of eternity, I — and presumably many others with me — would like to meet again " our friends the little birds." But will my half-tamed tits continue to eat plant-lice and my friend the wryneck feed on ants? Will lice and bugs and other vermin turn up again on the other side, but so transfigured that they will only exist in order that we may amuse ourselves by studying their lives and admiring them for the delicate and complicated organisms they actually are, even if their earthly habits render them a nuisance to us humans?

2

BUT in spite of all, to Professor Hallesby the *first* and real state of bliss is the perfect union with God which is attained in the next world. " What is all-important to the bride is to possess the bridegroom, not his gifts." When therefore the late Judge Dahl in his books presents his new religion — popularly called spiritualism — as an improved Christianity, and in particular as an improvement on Professor Hallesby's, then I am bound to say I prefer the Hallesby religion.

Most spiritualist books — at any rate most of those which have some circulation outside the community of the already converted — have been written in circumstances which cause ordinary people to feel a natural reluctance to attack them. The first one that came into my hands, Sir Oliver Lodge's *Raymond, or Life and Death,* was written by a father about a son who fell in the World War. His love for this lad was only equalled by his admiration, and so it makes *him* happy to believe " not merely that personality persists, but that its continued existence is more entwined with the life of every day than has been generally imagined; that there is no real breach of continuity between the dead and the living; and that the methods of intercommunion across what has seemed to be a gulf can be set going in response to the urgent demand of affection." [1]

One has the feeling that a connection of this sort through mediums and automatic writing is a sadly poor substitute for warm-hearted daily intercourse, and the descriptions of " life on the other side " appear dismally trivial — nevertheless one says to oneself, you cannot tell how you would take it if you lost one of your own children. But, for all that, it is difficult to imagine how people are constituted who are so entirely satisfied with their own belongings — their children and their own circle and surroundings — so convinced of the excellence of their personal aims and activities that they can suppose without a shudder that life will go on " developing " on the same lines from sphere to sphere — who are positively pleased with the idea that death is a trifling mat-

---

[1] *Raymond,* Introduction to Part II.

ter — not the end of all. Nor yet a catastrophe, terrible in that we have no experience, even of a spiritual nature, that has not come to us through the medium of our body, a medium from which we are now cut off — liberating in that we are now cut off from all that is unessential. Ludvig Dahl assures us that death is in reality " the passing to a form of life on a new wave-length, neither more nor less miraculous than earthly birth." [1] To call earthly birth a passing to a form of life on a new wave-length is, to say the least of it, an odd and not particularly apt way of putting it. An earthly birth is in any case a somewhat harrowing affair: if everything goes as it should, the mother shrieks and the infant shrieks too as it leaves its warm bath within the walls of the womb and slips into the dazzling light and the air which cools and dries its moist and tender skin, while it sprawls and struggles in a vain search for the walls that used to support it. — But it seems that a soul torn out of its old skin just jogs along on the same old round. To die is nothing.

Of Judge Dahl's books it may be said with even greater truth than of Lodge's *Raymond* that the joyful message of spiritualism is presented upon a background of the author's family bereavement, so that a reader who finds the message tasteless feels reluctant to express his opinion. For if these séances that he describes were really capable of consoling a father and mother who within a few years had lost two grown-up sons . . .

[1] *Vi overlever Döden (We Survive Death),* p. 53.

9

His books give one the impression of an altogether exceptional mutual affection prevailing in the author's family. All its members admire one another boundlessly, they hold together, have a language of their own, and a family likeness so marked that one has to read with the greatest attention if one is to know which member of the family, living or dead, happens to be speaking. The two dead lads are accompanied by a swarm of uncles and aunts, grandparents, brothers- and sisters-in-law, intimate friends of the family and acquaintances of every degree. All their talk is so much alike that one would think a single consciousness expressed itself through every one of them. They have their own jargon — a lavish use of pet names — mams and mims and paps and grannies and much more of the same sort. They call their séances " indescribably homelike "; they constantly have " marvellous experiences " and " delightful intermezzos "; they call each other " sweet " and use the same word of the things they hear and see. Another expression which the circle works to death is " little." One of the grandpas talks to " clever little Dagny " about his wife in a higher sphere, calling her " natty little mother." A friend of the family writes a letter through the medium, Fru Ingeborg, and alludes to it thus: " Well, little friend, I know you have received my unpretending little letter. If I had cared to task the little girl's strength more severely," and so on. A stranger, the hero of " a regular romance, a veritable ghost-story," to use the author's own expression, addresses this same medium as " you sweet little thing." Another stranger from the spirit world, a Dane who calls himself Per Lövbo, sends a message through Fru Ingeborg to another woman whom he constantly refers to as " the little lady," " my little friend." [1]

Everything that these deceased persons have to say about life on the other side shows moreover that it fulfils to an altogether surprising degree the wishes and hopes and ambitions of this particular family and clique. The spirit Ludvig has every reason to say that their existence is in a way extraordinarily similar to that which they had known on earth. " It makes me so indescribably happy, perhaps for the very reason that I was so fond of my earthly existence — that this life resembles it so closely, I mean." [2] To such an extent do these departed spirits find things to their taste that if they had been allowed to create heaven and earth for themselves, they could not have done it better. The rest of us poor sinners are often tempted to think that if God had consulted us when creating we might easily have suggested one or two improvements. But evidently the spiritualists are never exposed to temptations of this sort.

Now, of course it is no argument against the truth of spiritualism to say that I or anyone else should look upon survival as a monstrous idea if I held the belief that we were to survive in order to continue our existence in conditions which had anything in common with Judge

---

[1] *Livet efter Döden i nyt Lys (Life after Death in a New Light)*, pp. 213 ff.

[2] Ibid., p. 109.

Dahl's descriptions. The belief that after death human beings continue to live as spirits — if not for eternity, in any case for an indefinite period — is common to practically all peoples and races on earth. But that this belief should have resulted from man's insatiable nature, which demands more, more, more life and refuses to accept the idea of a final separation from all that he loves — this is one of those doctrinaire theories of which the nineteenth century was so fond. In reality some peoples have believed that after death the spirits go to a distant land where life is pleasant, while others have imagined the existence of the spirits to be miserably dreary and empty — and it looks as if the latter idea has been most prevalent among peoples who have not been in contact with Christian missionaries. And archæology and ethnography have a good deal to tell us about the precautions people have taken in all ages to prevent the dear departed from returning to their old haunts — but considerably less about any attempts to achieve communion with the dead, unless it were with the object of deriving some profit therefrom. People have believed in a life after death because they believed it to be a fact, whether pleasant or otherwise. In this they showed more sense than many people of the present day who declare that they don't believe in a life after death because they have no desire to live after death — or something to that effect. Which is not an argument, but a naïveté.

So for that matter there might easily be another world resembling that described by Judge Dahl — though in such a world I should feel like a fly that had dropped into a bowl of syrup, and it is an awful thought that one would have to flounder in the syrup *in sæcula sæculorum*. However, what makes most people outside a certain narrowly constricted circle regard with absolute incredulity the spiritualist revelations from a happy land beyond the grave is the fact that this happy land corresponds far too closely to the ideas of a certain type of humanity about a land of Cockaigne. This type occurs almost exclusively among what is called the upper middle class and among those old enough to have been moulded intellectually by the currents of the last third of the nineteenth century. It is obvious that these people's children, when they converse " from beyond " with their elders, share the opinions and tastes and ideals of their parents in a quite astonishing degree. One is instinctively tempted to ask: were these young people, Raymond Lodge and his friends, the children of Judge Dahl's circle, while yet alive, so absolutely united in soul and mind with their elders that the natural tension between the generations never asserted itself on any point? That they *lived* in harmony with their parents I am quite willing to believe — that is not so difficult in homes where culture and goodwill prevail. But did they really *feel* and *think* in such absolute unison with them?

The spiritualist world of ideas is dominated by the evolutionary optimism of last century, when those classes of the population that one was accustomed to call

I   3

the educated public had heard a good deal about evolution. When biological research produced evidence that the more differentiated forms of life had developed from simpler forms and described these as " higher " and " lower " respectively, no *moral* estimation was implied. And we may be sure that the naturalist himself had no intention of suggesting that the development from the Silurian fish to the cod and halibut on his dinner-table meant that these fish had advanced " nearer, my God, to Thee," or that it was more moral and noble to be a bird than to be a fish. But it was precisely something of this sort that the educated public took out of the doctrine of evolution — they made for themselves a kind of substitute for religion, a view of life according to which evolution meant progress in a moral sense, and " higher forms " in every field meant forms which from their point of view were more profitable. Well-meaning souls who were quite pleased with themselves and tolerably content with their lot felt an immense encouragement in being permitted to believe that by degrees all men would become as admirable as they were and would live in equally admirable circumstances — and moreover we should all be better and better off day by day.

This evolutionary optimism has been translated by the spiritualists to a world which is assumed to be awaiting us beyond death. The spirit Eva, a relative of the Dahl family, tells us in *Livet efter Döden i nyt Lys* (p. 193) : " Our circles consist of several social classes, if I may use the expression. And we have small — let me call them towns, where everything is arranged more or less in the same way as in a well-regulated town on your side, with houses, parks, streets, churches, and lecture-halls, with animals and with people. . . . It is all so pleasant and agreeable here. Facilities for all kinds of recreation and full opportunities for following one's interests." " Naturally [!] we have amusements *en masse,*" the same Eva informs us. Only they must not be carried to excess. Otherwise the development of the spirits to the " higher spheres " is accomplished by the good old means in which the evolutionary believers used to have such touching confidence: education, ranging from kindergarten instruction for the little child spirits to specialized studies for the undergraduate spirits. The more learned and highly cultivated spirits (such as, for instance, one of the Dahl family's grandfathers) give lectures. But in addition the spirits have opportunities of improving their minds through travel, through artistic gratification and all the approved and time-honoured methods of intellectual culture.

In a way there is something touching in this confiding appetite of the spiritualists for all the material good things of earth. It does not occur to them that anyone might think them good enough for a time — for we know that we shall not enjoy them for so very many years. If this were not so we should soon have had enough of them. But the spiritualists evidently think you can't have too much of a good thing. The Dahl family listen with delight to an episode, " a tiny one, but so sweet ": the spirits Ludvig and Skat are on a visit to a higher sphere, and on their way to divine service in a magnificent marble hall they discover some violets by the wayside, their own beloved violets from Seirsborg, the villa at home in Fredrikstad! [1]

Should we be able to realize the marvel of spring if we did not know in our inmost soul that one spring would be the last *we* should see? In the legends of sunken continents, Atlantis and Lemuria, there lives our racial memory of the transformations in the earth's surface as a result of which " our beautiful country to which God has bound us by so many ties " is relatively brand-new and young, and the glacial pressure of future ice ages will perhaps reknead it, and cataclysms will break up the mountain chains into new forms. Measured by the standard of human life it is immensely old, and yet it is but a passing smile on the face of the globe. All that we know through our physical senses is matter which is continually changing its form. Our spirit, looking for causes and effects in the eternal play of transformation, has felt certain that this play is directed by persons or a person whom our thinking and searching ego resembled in some way or other and was related to. So it has been as far back as we know anything of human history on earth, and religion is our relation to these causes or this cause which stands above matter and deals with it as it pleases. Religion is our relation to the supernatural.

[1] *Vi overlever Döden*, pp. 233 ff.

I 6

3

THE PHENOMENA which spiritualists cite as evidence for
their special doctrine of life after death have in themselves no connection with religious problems properly
so called. Of course it is possible that supernatural beings — intelligences existing and operating independ-
ently of matter — may be involved to some extent. But
everything that has hitherto been reported from spiritualist séances has been such as to admit of an entirely
natural explanation — only at present we do not know
how the phenomena occur, and our knowledge of the
forces in operation is too slight. It is certain, for instance, that many primitive races possess powers which
have been stunted or destroyed in our forms of civilization; they are none the less natural for that. But as
things are, most of us must nevertheless have had experiences, have witnessed phenomena, which I am quite
willing to call occult in the sense of mysterious or
inexplicable. What for instance are " fetches " — the
wraiths or doubles of living persons? I am ashamed to
say I have never made any effort to find out, though
many of my relations have had very distinct fetches, and
I myself have once or twice " seen " people some time
before they came. But I must say it has never occurred
to me to class such inexplicable occurrences as I myself
have experienced — warnings, dreams that prove true,
visual or aural phenomena which come under the head

of what is popularly called spooks — as connected with anything supernatural, still less with religion.

Moreover the problem whether we survive death or not is not in itself necessarily one of religious interest — the point is *how* we survive it. A soul that in mystical ecstasy has known communion with the Deity has had its religious experience whether it dies when the body dies or continues to live for a time, or for eternity. We have other reasons for believing that this mystical communion between spirit and spirit is more than an isolated experience, once for all — a foretaste of an eternal life in bliss. The saints who have experienced it are agreed that in reality they cannot express what they experienced, since no one, not even themselves, possesses the means of expressing other than sensorial experiences. So mystics of all confessions are unanimous in reminding us that it is only through analogies that they can tell us anything at all of this. More often than not they have borrowed their images from the relation between bride and bridegroom — from the highest erotic ecstasy, in which one being yearns to lose itself in the other. And the mystics themselves have continually reminded us that the figurative language of bridal mysticism *is* no more than figurative.

The religious teaching of spiritualism is puritanically free from bridal mysticism. And in general the Protestant communities have tended to reject such passionate outbursts of divine love with scandalized prudery — in spite of the fact that they break out again whenever any large-scale revivalist movement relights the fires of religion on Protestant territory. But spiritualism, in so far as it is connected with historical Christianity, continues the development which Sören Kierkegaard lashed in *Öjeblikket (The Moment)* — away from the New Testament's preaching of the great and terrible adventure of life or death for all eternity, towards a kind of comfortable, utilitarian faith which allows of agreeable social intercourse, pleasant emotions, and high jinks. Spiritualists are content with the idea that they will only attain personal contact with God after travelling through many spheres — the impatient yearning for God which naturally borrows its imagery from erotics is not to be found among them. The conception of God is never that of a bridegroom, but of a good breadwinner.

It therefore strikes us as curious that Judge Dahl, among others, should maintain that spiritualism is to act as a counterpoise to " the spirit of materialism." Everything that has extension in space and occupies room is matter — if one thing feels less solid to our senses than another, that does not make it more " spiritual." Diamonds, coal, and coal-smoke are equally material. I admit I am not clear whether the marble halls in which the deceased listen to lectures, the cards with which they play bridge, the food that sustains them, and the charming clothes they go about in are to be regarded as composed of a sort of " sublimated matter " — in which case they are just as material as Uranienborg Church, my patience cards, and the beefsteaks one eats in the restaurant. Or are the deceased real spirits — existing without taking up room in space — and do they only enjoy the ideas of marble halls, bridge games, good food, and so on? In either case they are not less but more materialistic than the most hardboiled materialist who does not believe in the existence of spirits, or human spirits in any case, except as confined in matter, and who is content to enjoy the good things of this world and to suffer its troubles for seventy years or so. The majority of confessed materialists would doubtless decline with thanks if an offer were made to them to live this life for seven times seventy years — materialism as a view of life has at any rate the advantage of teaching us how quickly our capacity for enjoying material good things becomes dull and worn. Were it not for the fear that death might take them from us before we were ready to let them go, we should probably not be capable of loving those men and women who at some point of our lives were our dearest and have been our nearest through generations. For in reality it is uncomfortable to think how tired of one another we can get — even parents of their children, and children of their parents — unless people continually renew, through a religious relation to a God or gods, their powers of living with their fellow-humans. No doubt we should all find each other intolerable if we had to live together eternally — unless eternal life were above all else communion with a source of power which unceasingly strengthens and renews us — sanctifies us, to use the theological expression.

Probably some will say that in any case spiritualism is an idealistic materialism. And of course one may call it that — since its spokesmen are idealists in their own fashion. But so are most people, if by ideals we understand wish-fulfilment dreams, and this has now become the meaning of the word in ordinary speech, although most people understand by idealist a dreamer whose wishes are more or less coloured by altruism. Like most materialistic idealists or idealistic materialists, the spiritualists assume that in the happy land they picture to themselves everyone must find everything he can reasonably demand for his welfare.

This, however, is the point where spiritualism really becomes blasphemous — when it declares its readiness to " rehabilitate Christianity " and revise the Scriptures, purifying them of all statements that do not fit into the new comfortable, enlightened, and happy religion.

Many will doubtless think we need not trouble very much about what the spiritualists teach. They may of course be fairly numerous in the English-speaking countries, in Denmark, Norway, and so on; nevertheless they all belong to a definite type of bourgeois mentality. And whatever we may think of the bourgeois society's prospects of survival, on one point there can be no doubt: the bourgeois ideal belongs to the past. Regarded from this point of view, there is something almost touching in the curiously aloof and washed-out way in which the spiritualists treat the problem of evil, on the rare occasions when they think they ought to converse with the spirits on some other topic than the welfare of the family and how pleasant things are on the other side.

A characteristic account is given twice over in Judge Dahl's books.[1] The spirit Ludvig tells us in a series of séances about an " expedition to the lower spheres " on which he was sent together with his brother Skat and some other spirits of the same degree of goodness. For it seems there *is* a kind of underworld and it is the abode of those deceased persons whose nature is of an " ethically baser type, among whom egoism, arrogance, desire, or passion has gained the upper hand " (*Vi overlever Döden*, p. 86). It was characteristic of nice, refined Norwegians of last century that " passion " was always taken to mean something unseemly and immoral. Consciously, at any rate, they knew nothing of sacred passion or moral passion — noble emotions were never imagined as fiery, their warmth was that of a cosy room or a well-lined nest. — However, these base, earth-bound existences infest human beings and cause them to commit evil deeds. For an infinite number of the crimes committed on earth are due to these horrible parasites from the morasses of the underworld. Therefore the human race must be set free from this nightmare. — We are given to understand that it is Christ (!) who tells the spirits this. It appears they are first summoned to a sort of divine service in a marble hall, situated in a higher sphere — then the roof is rent asunder and Christ descends into the congrega-

[1] *Död, hvor er din Brodd (Death, Where Is Thy Sting?)*, pp. 155 ff., repeated in *Vi overlever Döden*, pp. 239 ff.

tion as a radiant figure. The whole thing strikes one as a recollection of some baroque altarpiece. Christ then provides the spirits with some shining crosses which are to serve as mascots during their visit to the lower spheres. And then these spirits, who obviously belong to the higher social classes in the spirit city — according to what has been revealed by Eva — are sent on a kind of midnight mission to save the spirits of the slum quarters beyond the veil.

The similarity between this world and the other is positively uncanny. If anything has contributed to bring Christianity into discredit it is just this kind of missionary effort — on the part of sincerely kind and zealous clergymen and lay preachers, chatty parsons' wives and philanthropic parish workers, who between whiles were able to withdraw to their good homes where they could repose in Spartan or comfortable surroundings, in any case among people of their own set whom they loved and respected, and could occupy themselves with edifying relaxation and the cultivation of their higher interests. In general these missionary efforts were undoubtedly undertaken with the very best intentions, often demanding immense resolution, in fear and trembling. On the whole they have certainly done more harm than good. For it cannot be denied that there are spheres in which it is of little use to work unless one has a saint's capacity for self-criticism.

As here, so on the other side. Two or three poor souls — weaker natures — see that the missionaries anyhow mean well by them and accept the proffered help. But apart from these they get the reception which slum-dwellers are apt to give self-satisfied visitors, so far as they dare. They venture into one of the underworld's places of entertainment. There was some delirious music, and it sounded as if dancing was going on both above and below the room they were in, which was furnished with a roulette-table and chairs and tables by the walls. " On entering we were met with coarse laughter and tumul-tuous applause. . . . They obviously took us for new-comers from earth. They wanted to know what crimes we could boast of having committed, since we had found our way to this place. They also asked whether we were aware that it was still possible to take part in pleasures on earth, by simply attaching ourselves as parasites to weak individuals who were susceptible to influence. They told us with enthusiasm that they practised evil for evil's sake, and vindicated with heartfelt conviction the claims of evil to parity with good " (*Vi overlever Döden*, p. 241). Spirits of the underworld also have " amuse-ments *en masse* " — precisely of the kind which used to make respectable people shudder in my childhood. They were regarded as manifestations of extreme moral corruption.

Now, it is obvious that this band of missionaries would be ill fitted to try conclusions with more danger-ous forms of evil — with the far more numerous souls who do evil because they are afraid, or because they be-lieve, or persuade themselves that they believe, they are promoting a good cause by doing evil. — In February 1933 the spirit Ludvig tells his family (*Död, hvor er din Brodd,* p. 111) that he and his brother have been entrusted with a " confidential mission." And on March 30, 1933 he is able to announce that he has had a great many interesting experiences. " Queer state of affairs in the world today. It will require immense efforts to prevent people from making yet more blunders. . . . Phew, what a lot of insanity we have seen! . . . We have flown all round Europe, so to speak. We have been to The Hague, to Geneva, to Paris, to the Slav countries, to Germany and Russia — a kaleidoscope of situations and episodes. Without a doubt intervention from above is more necessary than ever before. It might so easily happen that the world caught fire once more. The struggle with and against men's free will is a hard one. . . . Well, unfortunately it is difficult to give you any proper account of these things, partly because many of our experiences are confidential, but also because it would be in itself an almost hopeless task." The spirits keep on for a good while with communications of this sort, which would rouse the scorn of any boy with a moderately developed instinct for reality if he read them in his school paper.

We are told in *Vi her!* [1] that the spirit Ragnar is studying law in the other world, for " it sometimes happens even in our Paradise that somebody does something

---

[1] This book has been published in an English translation with the title *We Are Here* (1931).

which is not right, and so we have our tribunal," with prosecuting and defending counsel. Ragnar is already promoted to be an advocate on probation, and his brother assures us that he is " a sweet defending counsel." We do not get the impression, however, that the administration of justice in the higher spheres is of a nature to inspire much confidence.

But the author, Judge Dahl, who, be it remembered, has a long life behind him, including many years on the bench, writes on his own account (*Vi her!* pp. 23–4): " To rely on God's never-resting care, as a child relies on its mother, this is the faith which we need and which moves mountains. Add to this faith an urge and a willingness to do God's will, corresponding to the good child's obedience to mother and father, and you have the whole of religion. It is as simple as that according to the new message. It *was* as simple as that according to Christ's own preaching on earth. The doctrine of God's *wrath* is what has made religion complicated and difficult among men. But this doctrine is false, says the new message. God looks upon men with a smile — the eironeia smile — not in wrath. . . . Have you read Andersen's story ' Heart's Sorrow '? It tells of a widow's pugdog that died, and then of the pug's grave being shown by little boys who charged a breeches button for admission, and lastly the story tells of a little girl crying." She had no breeches button — and that was her heart's sorrow, as deep as that of many grown-ups. " We saw it from above — and, seen from above, this like so many of our own and others' sorrows — well, we can smile at them! That is the story, and he who does not understand it may take shares in the widow's tannery.

" Do you understand it? Very well, then you also understand God's eironeia smile. *He* looks upon *us* from above — and He loves us and smiles."

We may well imagine that God does not see as we see, and also that discarnate spirits view the misery of this world otherwise than ourselves who are in the midst of it. But there is something preternaturally cheerless in the idea of spirits having travelled through Europe in March 1933 and seen as it were the sum of human suffering, fear, distrust, injustice, distress, false fanaticism, and misused enthusiasm, and then telling about it with childish complacency — when the same spirits are still so taken up with their own material welfare (sublimated, to be sure), and when all the trifles that concern their own home circle still mean as much to them as when they were living in their former skins.

Contrasted with this, Professor Hallesby's faith is after all far more of a grown-up person's religion, in spite of all subjectivity and narrowing influences of environment. He has at any rate some knowledge of human beings as something more than mere domesticated animals, and he knows that if God is our Father and we are His children, we are not His infants in arms; God permits us to become grown-up children — and it sometimes happens that grown-up children turn their backs on their father and their home for good. When spiritualists assure us that " good " will finally be victorious all along the line, assuming them to mean by this that evil will be deprived of its very existence, they postulate a God not as a father but as a tyrant, even if He is conceived in the likeness of a benevolent universal paterfamilias.

In common with all other religion-makers who announce their products as a " development of Christianity," the spiritualists talk about Jesus' " simple teaching " — after men have quarrelled for nineteen hundred years and even been burnt at the stake over the meaning of this simplicity — and about His " gentle " doctrine of love. I myself have never been able to guess where people get this image of the ever " gentle " Jesus from — unless indeed they accept a Church whose claim it is that Christ still speaks to men through her. The Church has *emphasized* Jesus' tenderness for all who suffer and toil — that is to say the majority — and she has reminded us of His blessing all those who lack the capacity for making their fortune in this world. But she has not on that account suppressed other traits of the New Testament's portrayal of Christ — the terrible outbursts of divine indignation, His saying that He came not to bring peace but a sword, and to send fire upon the earth, to separate parents and children and children-in-law, so that he who would be His disciple must be able to hate his own parents if necessary, and even his most intimate friends may be glad if they are not scandalized at him. — The conception of Jesus as a frail and kindly visionary with no knowledge of human nature as it really is (it is odd to find that Pär Lagerkvist has adopted this egregiously bourgeois Jesus-cliché in *The Hangman*), or as an amiable young preacher with a special talent for touching the hearts of women's unions, must have arisen in middle-class circles of last century, which held fast to a certain highly diluted Christian tradition. It was taken for granted that love of one's neighbour and the belief in the perfectibility of all men were peculiarly Christian ideas — which was right as far as it went. But the traditional veneration for the name of Jesus was not disturbed by any suspicion that the neighbourly love of Jesus Christ and His ideas about men's perfectibility — sanctification — might differ fundamentally from their own rational views on these matters. The long, shadowy procession of so-called " historical Jesuses " represents in fact the emotionally coloured reluctance to abandon the religious feelings of their childhood among people who believed that Christianity in a historical sense was played out — and who at the same time were trying to construct for themselves a Christ figure whose behaviour and sayings might be reconciled with their own " *nihil obstat.*"

It is natural that a generation which regarded itself as Christian on such assumptions as these should be followed by a generation which is entirely dechristianized. Children may inherit the faith of their forefathers, and this faith may be doubly precious and sacred to them because it is that of their forefathers. But against the subjective opinions and the sentiments of their parents most children will react — this is the order of nature.

When therefore the spiritualists feel called upon to reform Christianity and set up their new message in opposition to Professor Hallesby's interpretation of Christianity, based as the latter is on English-Calvinistic-Puritanical and Old-Lutheran Jehovah-complexes, I cannot imagine that they will make any converts outside the circles which have already refused to follow Christianity's urgent appeal to spiritual conflict, and which content themselves with religion as consolation. — Even in the view of the narrowest orthodoxy God is nevertheless God, and Christ the incarnate God and Chief. It is unthinkable that any grown-up human soul that has experienced a personal relation with Him can feel it to be anything but blasphemy when God is reduced to a sort of cornucopia on the top of a sort of cosmic wedding-cake.

(1935)

D. H. LAWRENCE

It may safely be said that the whole of Lawrence's production was autobiographical to an even greater extent than is the case with all imaginative writing. For one thing, his life from his very youth was a ceaseless struggle against the pulmonary complaint of which he died, at the early age of forty-five. Thus he was debarred more than most people from forgetting himself, were it only for a moment, in admiration or ecstasy over some person or thing. In the last years of his life he produced a series of poems on animal and plant motives, some of them of rare beauty. They are a perfect expression of man's primeval instinct for picturing his own spiritual life through flowers and tortoises and mountains and heraldic figures — through anything non-human. Finally his poetical imagination carried him into chaos and cosmos. In mystical speculations Lawrence applied himself to ancient astrological ideas about the twelve signs of the zodiac, which were supposed to " govern " the various parts and organs of the human body — of his body.

Sons and Lovers, however, is autobiographical in a more direct sense than the rest of Lawrence's writing. His sister, Ada Lawrence, has made superabundantly clear the exact correspondence between " Paul Morel's " story and the life of David Herbert Lawrence in adolescence and youth. And she has illustrated her book with photographs of Lawrence's parents and family, of houses and places which under slightly disguised names are the scene of action in Lawrence's novels and tales. So that anyone may convince himself that, seen with the eyes of an outsider, it was an unspeakably dull and ordinary, but entirely respectable little world that Lawrence grew up in.

His mother and sisters called him Bert. — In English comic papers " Bert " is the stock name for the Cockney youth, the amorous counter-jumper, the pale and skinny errand-boy who revels in wish-fulfilment dreams about ardent love and desperate deeds as he sits at the cinema gulping down pictures of shadowy film stars' adventures, or works himself up yelling with the crowd at a football match. And there have been some who would like to reduce Lawrence to a rebellious Bert, breaking windows to let air into the stuffy, taboo-ridden homes of the respectable lower middle class.

His sister tells us that as a little boy Lawrence actually was subject to fits of tears, and if his mother asked what he was crying for he only cried worse: " I don't know." Over-sensitive to changes of mood and ill humour on the part of those who surrounded him, the child felt, before he was conscious of it, that he was growing up on a battle-ground.

His mother, Lydia Beardsall, had been a school-teacher. She hungered and thirsted after all that in her young days was meant by intellectuality and idealism; she had a strongly developed sense of responsibility and a fanatical respect for herself. Then she fell in love with a miner, Arthur Lawrence, and married him. Later on she could never forgive him for this love-match, which shut her off from all she desired to get out of life. The husband seems on the whole to have been a happy, easy-going nature. His capacity for enjoying life had not been impaired by the hardships of his childhood — he had worked in the coal-mines since the age of seven. He did not possess that kind of self-absorption which is a necessary component of all social advancement, but he was well supplied with another sort of self-confidence: he was proud of being strong and good-looking, a lik-able fellow with a cheerful spirit which was not to be repressed by poverty and hard work. And then he was to find out that his charming, refined wife was not so well pleased with him as to be able to reconcile herself to the conditions to which he had introduced her. She never managed to feel at home among the miners and their wives, in the ugly, dirty little towns of the coal-mining district round Nottingham. And she never allowed the pressure of poverty and her surroundings to make her abandon the fight for her ideals. She fought for her children — they at any rate should have as much as possible of all that she had been deprived of; they should belong to her people, not to their father's. *He* was the enemy in their mother's eyes. Perplexed and humiliated, he had recourse to all kinds of deplorable shifts in order to assert himself. She was a rigid abstainer — so he sat at the public-house with his mates till late at night. When he came home, " slightly fuddled and pleasantly apologetic," and his wife received him with freezing indignation, he turned brutal. Among the children's memories was that of being constantly waked up by the stormy disputes of their parents — they lay in the dark and heard the voices warring in the room below. — The tragic part of it was that the husband was really a home-loving man in his way. His daughter tells us how handy he was at fixing up anything that was broken in the house. He loved to have his children standing round him as he repaired the alarm-clock or patched their shoes; that was his way of playing with them. " If, instead of wanting the impossible from him, we had tried to interest ourselves in the things for which he really cared, we should have been spared many unhappy and sordid scenes," Ada Lawrence writes. But the children took their mother's part fanatically. This was natural — they had to thank her industry, her sense of order, both spiritual and material, for all they knew of well-being and home comfort. She backed their efforts to improve themselves, socially and intellectually. No doubt their father had intended from the first that the boys might start in the coal-mine, the daughters go out into service,

as soon as they were old enough. Later on he took great
pride in his talented children. And it is singularly painful to read what his daughter writes of him after her
mother's death. He was asked why he did not marry
again, and he replied: " I've had one good woman — the
finest woman in the world, and I don't want another."
But so long as she was alive the children excluded their
father from their life with their mother. He had his re-
venge, unreflecting creature of instinct that he was, by
doing all he could to pain this " swell " family of his —
adopting rude manners and undesirable habits, this man
who had once been so proud of his fine healthy appearance. But it is certainly due in the first place to the boy's
reaction to his father that Lawrence later on showed
such a persistent tendency to romanticize manliness.
In his books he constantly talks about " the strong in-
domitable male." With the shyness and pride and bold-
ness of a wild animal he woos and wins and loves and
withdraws into his silent and haughty isolation, as mys-
teriously manly as any figure to be found in the sloppi-
est of young ladies' novels. Lawrence had been brought
up to look down on his father, but his father was the
only person in the home over whom his mother did not
hold sway — he both defied her openly and managed to
evade her control.

In his flights of fancy on the subject of psychoanalysis
and the subconscious, Lawrence wrote with unsparing
bitterness of the husband who fails his wife and of the
wife who in her disappointment bestows all her affec-

tion on her sons. She thus conquers the finest element of their personality, the flowering of the boys' spiritual eroticism. When the time comes for them to have actual erotic experience, they have nothing but remnants to give away to other women. — There is now available a whole literature about D. H. Lawrence's life, written for the most part by ladies who can boast of having known him more or less well. As Compton Mackenzie aptly remarks, the dead Lawrence has suffered the same fate as the living Orpheus: to be torn to pieces by his female followers. It was, by the way, a male " friend " of Lawrence, Middleton Murry, who let loose the whole flood of personal reminiscences about the dead poet. In a somewhat nauseous and turgid book Murry tried to reduce the mysterious quality in Lawrence to so simple a supposition as his alleged impotence. The chorus of protesting women's voices makes it clear in any case that the enigmatic element in Lawrence's genius is not to be explained quite so easily. After all we have been told about him — by friends male and female and by Lawrence's widow — about the irresistible charm of his manner, about his terrible unsociableness, about his candour and his disingenuousness — there still remains something mystical about his person. But finally the girl who had been his companion and confidante during the years when he was feeling his way to his own individuality — Miriam he calls her in *Sons and Lovers* — wrote a little book about her relations with the lad Lawrence. Time after time Lawrence returns to this Miriam figure — a girl who detests the sexual element in love, but who wants to love a man spiritually and to possess his soul and his talent. Against these ideas, then, " Miriam " herself finally protested. She was a perfectly normal and healthy young woman and had never thought or felt that there was any opposition between the physical and the spiritual in love. It was Lawrence who was uncertain, who dared not embark on a real love-affair with her, because his mother was jealous and he was dominated by her, and because his sisters did all they could to separate their brother and his girl friend. When at last the lad tried to transform their friendship into a love-affair, it was too late. The girl had *turned* cold, from long waiting and from humiliation.

Mrs. Lawrence must have perceived at an early stage that " Bert " possessed more than ordinary ability, though she can hardly have grasped either its nature or its extent. He did a little painting as a boy, he won a scholarship which qualified him for a higher school, he became a teacher, he began to write — and of course this was all to the good. Step by step her children were freeing themselves from the social surroundings in which she had been imprisoned. But if they were forced to marry, as the saying is, while still quite young, why, then their whole future would be ruined. And in that no doubt most sensible people would agree with her.

Her son was just able to place an advance copy of his first book, *The White Peacock,* in his mother's hands, but she died without having read it. And then he had to try to work his way out of the environment which had wrapped him round like a mother's womb. When some time later he gave up his position as teacher and left England with the lady he married a couple of years afterwards — that is, as soon as her divorce was made absolute — he thought he was born anew for a life under more spacious skies and was to breathe the air of other worlds. But so forcible had been the pressure of his home on the mind of the abnormally sensitive lad that D. H. Lawrence bore to his dying day the stamp of the influences that act upon young Paul Morel in *Sons and Lovers.*

The after-effects of the feud between his parents reverberate through all his writings. Lawrence, who made himself the prophet of an altogether mystical sexual religion — the " regeneration by sex " of England and of the white race in general — describes the sexual relation as a war to the death between man and woman. This ground-motive recurs incessantly in his work, infinitely varied — the man in revolt, the man in flight from the woman who tries to tamper with him, to kill and devour him; woman is a fury who rages against man for reducing her to subjection and who despises him when he fails to do so. The latent dread of the horrors of sexual warfare culminates with Lawrence in scenes of a savage, uncanny beauty, unlike anything else that has been written of the primitive dread of life — scenes like that of the final chapter of *The Rainbow,* where Ursula Bragwen meets with a mob of untethered horses in a field. The incomparably lifelike description of this troop of horses, galloping, halting, and circling again in a thundering trot round the terrified girl, becomes a symbol of all life's obscure and overpowering impulses; and Ursula's fear, that of everyone's sense of horror and impotence under the dominance of these impulses. This runs like a leading motive through all his poetry — culminating in the imaginative and moving verses about the tortoises that he used as sacred symbols of life's crucifixion in the torment of sex. Lawrence is seldom convincing when he tries to force the creatures born of his fancy to realize his own gospel of a new and saving kind of abandonment — a dark and mystical communion of the blood which is just as much the expression of the human instinct of death and destruction as of the will to life. But Lawrence dreamed of a sexual act in which the individuals die from their old ego and are reborn to a new life, each as master of his own soul, but united with his mate in profound tenderness, saved from all lust of power involved in sexual feeling, cleansed of all the elements of petty vanity which are a part of all erotics, but with their manly or womanly self-consciousness intensified. It was something of this sort that he wished to believe in. But the people who live in his books are in everlasting revolt against his new religion — irreclaimably timid, bitter, and suspicious men and women who are incapable of abandoning themselves to another human being without regretting it and immediately trying to recover themselves. This is true in particular of his most discussed book, *Lady Chatterley's Lover*. This book gave great offence when it came out. The majority of those scandalized were undoubtedly in good faith in explaining that what scandalized them was that Lawrence had tendentiously put into print a number of expressions which can have a neutral value only in the minds of very dull or sexually exhausted individuals; to most people they are too highly charged with heterogeneous emotional values; they belong at the same time to the most intimate love-making and to the most elementary outbursts of rage. Unconsciously the feeling of offence went far deeper, at any rate with many people. They felt how intolerably tragic were the naked descriptions of two human beings who in their embraces are trying to crush out of themselves their unbounded bitterness at their own erotic disappointments in the past and the immeasurable hatred they have gathered up in previous love-affairs. We may call the tendency of *Lady Chatterley's Lover* immoral, just as we may say the same of any book whose object it is to relate an untruth, however honestly the untruth may be expressed, or however it may be candied in the sugar of morality. But Lawrence simply could not be untrue to his vision; he could not allow Connie Chatterley and her lover to *be* reborn in any blood-communion. The novel does not end with their bringing any peace to each other. The most we can say is that they arrive at a sort of armistice — in the hope that this may end in peace.

He has a Balaam's ass inside him, Lawrence writes in another connection. " When I try to turn my travelling nose westwards, *grazie!* he won't budge. So, after vainly shoving and prodding the ass of my unwilling spirit, I have given up." In reality these words are typical of the relation between tendency and vision in Lawrence's writing.

For a visionary is what he was, and a poet of genius. But his own wish was to be a prophet, a saviour of the world, a Messiah. His passionately antichristian attitude was due above all to the fact that the figure of Jesus stood in his way. True, he and his brothers and sisters during the whole of their childhood and adolescence had been obliged every Sunday to attend three services besides Sunday school in the dissenting chapel to which his parents belonged. So it was natural enough that he should identify Christianity with the strict puritanism which dominated that place of worship. And he never got away from these impressions; he carried on the war against the maternal Bethel. But the new flesh-and-blood religion he sought to found bore the fundamental stamp of the unsmiling solemnity of his childhood's religion: when he strips men and women of their clothes and exposes the secret places of the body he is as serious as a priest at the sacrificial stone. In the end he fabled that Jesus Himself had been converted to his, Lawrence's, religion — he makes the crucified and risen Saviour renounce His errors and acknowledge that not His but Lawrence's way of salvation is the right one.

4 3

And he makes the discovery that the Revelation of John is in reality a pre-Lawrencian prophecy, an ancient pagan evidence of his own cosmology — John, like some kind of early Christian sectarian preacher, had merely tampered with the texts and stuffed them full of his own sanctimonious phraseology.

But no matter what he wrote — novels, short stories, poetry, essays, letters, travels — in his hands the subjects became new and his own property in a curious way. Like ore that has been heated in the furnace and comes out gleaming with unsuspected colours, bright and dark, the English language is fused in his burning brain and leaves his forge resmelted, with new and wonderful values. Infinitely susceptible to all sensuous impressions, Lawrence had felt from his boyhood in the very marrow of his soul the opposition between life, organic matter, and dead inorganic masses. The country surrounding his home is charming — pretty-pretty perhaps some would call it. But Lawrence absorbed it and identified himself with the life of the little wild animals and the flowers and trees and the life of the river under its banks. Even the refuse of life — dead leaves and manure in the farmyard of Miriam's rustic home, straw and haycocks — belongs to life as distinguished from dead inorganic things — the cancerous sores of coal-mines and railways on the green countryside, the eruption of workmen's dwellings, rows of houses built of ugly blackened brick. This opposition is lively even in his first book, *The White Peacock,* which deals more with a landscape and an old farm than with the people who live there. And in *Lady Chatterley's Lover,* which is in a way Lawrence's testament — or at any rate one of them — what is unforgettable is the description of the little copse where the lovers meet. A spot of nature besieged on every side by mines and slag-heaps, surrounded by railway lines — the night around it glowing with reflections from the works. The faun, Mellors, is forced into the defensive. He tries to defend his own and Connie Chatterley's lives against the mechanization of existence and against the cerebral activity of them both, which he fears, holding it to be the origin of all that is mechanical and bloodless and grey in the world and in human souls. Against the intellectual, Lawrence sets up the Panic in men; this is the source which sustains life in fear and in joy. Lawrence, who wished to be Messiah, wished also to be Pan.

He was egocentric like most sick people, but his ego was sufficiently elastic to absorb people he met and foreign countries and new skies — and yet he always carried with him the England that had been his native soil. It was this England that he saw slipping down into the melting-pot of the World War — and even today there is no one who can say exactly how much of it was lost in the fiery ordeal and how much has survived, substantially the same though cast into new forms. Then he set out on journeys all over the world to find people and places which might represent the object of his dreams — the primitive, unworn, red-blooded. He found them nowhere — he was not at home among the dusky natives of

Ceylon nor among Australian colonists, Polynesians, nor dancing Indians in Mexico. The contact with foreign conditions seems in itself always to have troubled Lawrence — except when he was living in Italy; but then Italy has been for centuries the home of the Englishman's longing and the land of his dreams. It is significant in this connection that in Italy he wrote a number of his most beautiful poems to the dead mother who had fostered his longing for travel and who herself had never been able to see the land of her desire. But with his own hypersensitive nerves he was revolted by the reptilian lack of sympathy he thought he could discern in the impenetrable dark eyes of really primitive peoples — though time after time he tries to accept and admire them, as he does in his tales from Mexico. It is true that he ended by attributing to the Mexicans a prophet and a revival of the local religion. In *The Plumed Serpent* a landowner founds a new faith which is composed of Lawrence's notions of ancient Mexican paganism, reinterpreted and improved according to his own mystical ideas. The book has an uncanny symptomatic interest in that it foreshadows the kind of religion-making which set in shortly after his death — the attempts to revive local pagan beliefs as they were apt to be popularized in accordance with the taste of a more or less cultured middle class for antiquarian romance and characterized by middle-class puritanical-materialistic idealism. — But by degrees, as he digested his impressions of the passing glories of this world, reliving in his mind what his eyes had told him, he fashioned from these impressions his incredibly hallucinatory art, which produces on the reader the effect of direct sensations of taste, vision, and feeling. With the same power of suggestion he makes the reader share his perception either of the landscape of his native district or of a single flower in a garden by the Mediterranean, a bathe in the Pacific on the coast of Australia, a morning in Mexico, or a steamer trip in midwinter from Sicily to Sardinia. If he fairly and squarely shocked a great part of the English public with his descriptions of erotic situations — and delighted another section of the same public with them — it was not because they were more " sensuous " than his pictures of flowers or animals or his travel scenes. His art acts directly upon the senses, whether it reproduces physical caresses or a night in a haycock or the motions of the berth one occupies on board a steamer in heavy weather. But it was natural that his art should give offence and alarm to a public accustomed to finding something literary or unlifelike and distant in the very tone of erotic descriptions, whether these were cynical or sentimental in treatment, tragic or pleasant or frivolous.

It was equally natural that Lawrence should feel himself wronged and finally persecuted: he was treated as a writer of immoral books, and perhaps no other author in the whole world had taken sex so desperately seriously as he! Lawrence the puritan saw red when anyone permitted himself to trifle frivolously or obscenely with the instincts which cause people to perform so many grotesque antics. In ages and among peoples which actually realized the freedom of speech that he believed would save humanity, Lawrence would have felt extremely ill at ease. In his berserk attacks on current English taboo-ideas he did not ask how such ideas arise. One explanation of them is the reaction against the guffaws of a period of free speech — even dogs and little children cannot bear to be laughed at; grown-up people hate it. And sometimes a taboo arises when people's imagination develops into compassion for the sufferings of others. Lawrence's mind swung ceaselessly between intense compassion for others and attempts to rebel against this tormenting fellow-feeling. This is connected with a quality which is both the strength and the weakness of Lawrence as a novelist. Few of the figures in his books have achieved the right to exist and act according to their own natures — more often than not Lawrence forces them to be and to act as he wishes. In dealing with his own creations he was like a mother — his own mother — who wishes to direct her offspring in everything. His knowledge of humanity is boundless. His knowledge of other persons than D. H. Lawrence is a great deal less.

But so many-sided was Lawrence and so intensely did he live his life that he becomes a representative figure — the man of mystery who symbolizes his civilization at the moment when it has reached a crisis. It is among other things a crisis of population and an economic crisis. In the language of mythology it means that the Phallus has lost its old significance as a religious symbol.

Since the days of Malthus the Europeans in any case had lost the ancient happy belief that fertility was unconditionally a good thing. When primitive races from time to time suspended the moral precepts of everyday life and celebrated orgies in order to make rain or assure a good harvest and a plentiful supply of game and domestic animals, it was because they confidently regarded their own life as a part of nature's economy. Crop failures and periods of famine were certainly not unknown to them, but it never occurred to them that some day mankind might be faced by the problem of the population exceeding its food supply to a possibly dangerous extent. The passionate attempts to emancipate sexuality from the service of propagation and to find its highest values under other aspects are first heard of precisely during the lifetime of Malthus. Not that they were influenced by his writing; this was rather the attempt of an intellectual to investigate the spectre that lurked behind the tendency of the poets. The romantics glorified love as the source of the loving souls' rapture — true love is that which makes the soul great and strong, causes the mind to soar, the heart to swell with noble feelings, gives wings to the imagination. This was the program — in reality most people probably contented themselves with pretending they were beautiful souls and loved in the correct romantic fashion. Poetry again reflected this sham romanticism — it came to concern itself with imitated emotions, sentimentality. Then the reaction set in — people were no longer willing to be told that they must please dress up and act a long charade before they could permit themselves sexual gratification. They were now to begin taking their sex naturally. — This reaction was no more disposed than the romantics had been to acknowledge that "Nature," so far as we humans can have any knowledge of the matter, has never had any object in driving individuals to the act of propagation except that they should propagate their species; after that the parent individuals can die, like the insects whose offspring do not require their care, or wear themselves out in bringing up their young, as among the higher animals. The desperate dilemma of the nineteenth century, which the twentieth has inherited, is precisely that with which Lawrence wrestles. As he says in his painfully beautiful, ithyphallic *Virgin Youth:*

> Traveller, column of fire,
> It is vain.
> The glow of thy full desire
> Becomes pain.

He himself never had a child. From the letters he wrote to her whom he afterwards married it appears as though in the early days of their connection he had wished for a child by her. She herself had three by a former marriage, a fact which hurt him both in his self-esteem as a man and in his, as it were, filial attitude towards the woman with whom he was to live; he wished at the same time to dominate and to be dominated in their relations. Soon, however, he grew so ill that it would have been unnatural if he had continued to wish for a child. And so he had to seek for another and more mystical meaning in the play of instincts. Indeed, it is very general for childless men to become pronouncedly erotic and given to erotic theorizing.

In opposition to the naïveté which looks forward to a new age simply because it is new, he was a voice crying in the wilderness. When simple souls call themselves the children of steel and concrete it is time to remind them of the yawning gulf fixed between life, which can beget life — whether by splitting up or pollination or copulation — and the whole inorganic world, which cannot reproduce itself. Steel and concrete are useful enough in their way. Nor, we may be sure, could Lawrence seriously imagine that modern technics could be got rid of. But if men appoint lifelessness and sterility as their adoptive parents, there is a danger that technics, instead of serving life, will destroy it. The widespread fear of the results of the mechanization of existence — a slow death from loss of heat — finds voice with Lawrence in poems and descriptions which burst like spouting blood from a severed artery, in intensely animated pictures of struggling life. And sometimes in reflections so obscure that they seem to express a dread the depth of which no one, not even Lawrence, dares to plumb. What can each individual human being make of himself, of his own life? — this is what will decide what the new age is to be like. Collectivism cannot in itself be the remedy for any distress, if the separate individuals are ciphers —

for nought plus nought will never equal anything but nought, however many million ciphers we may add.

Lawrence's perpetual harping on the sexual act, which to his sensitive soul meant communion, holy matrimony, the blood-contact between man and woman — between the two rivers, Euphrates and Tigris, which encircle Paradise, he says somewhere in his speculations upon the future destiny of the human race — was quite naturally misunderstood by the great mass of his fellow-countrymen; it had not yet occurred to them that their world might be threatened with freezing to death. It is another matter that the poet Lawrence continually put the words of the prophet Lawrence to shame. The new phallus-cult he sought to found no more brings peace and warmth in reality than it does to the eternally restless persons of his novels.

But the idea that the human blood is such a mystical source of power and warmth, the saving fluid, occurs naturally to men who are fighting against the fear of an ice age and of anything that depresses vitality. " For the blood is the substance of the soul, and of the deepest consciousness. It is by blood that we are: and it is by the heart and the liver that we live and move and have our being. In the blood, knowing and being, or feeling, are one and undivided: no serpent and no apple has caused a split." This is not a quotation from some modern German racial theologian; it was written by Lawrence in his *A Propos of Lady Chatterley's Lover*. — Much of what is happening in Europe today and yet more that will doubtless happen in the future are the brutal reaction of mass humanity to the problems which the exceptional man, the genius D. H. Lawrence, perceived and faced and fought against in his own way: in his writings, a great part of which in any case will pass into the heritage which our age will hand on to future generations.

(1935–8)

MARIE BREGENDAHL

Hendrik i Bakken (Henry of the Hill) was, so far as I know, Marie Bregendahl's first book. She called it " a picture." Perhaps the expression " pictures of country life " was already somewhat discredited at that time. For we were getting rather too many descriptive works of a certain kind — the museum type, one might call it. Sometimes they gave us information, valuable from a folklore point of view, of the customs, beliefs, and superstitions of past times; they contained elaborate descriptions of ancient styles of building and conscientiously catalogued the furniture of the old houses. But unfortunately these were inhabited by figures that had just as much life in them as the wax dolls one sees in folk-museums, designed to show how the old dresses were worn.

And the tale of Hendrik i Bakken and his wife is also handicapped by descriptions of the daily routine on an old Jutland farm in the '60's and '70's of last century. But already in this her first book we can trace Fru

Bregendahl's power of illuminating her scene as it were by irradiation from the life of the human beings who occupy it. With her the furniture and implements of the farms partake of the vital warmth of the people who wear them out. Hendrik's farm bears the stamp of Hendrik; the whole crowd of servants lives in uneasy reaction against the master, feeling the tension between him and his wife. They know that there is not much harm in Hendrik's unbearable manner, but it is just as unbearable for all that; they not only know that Mariane wishes her servants to be happy and comfortable — they guess that at heart she is still young. When she allows them to have a dance and stands food and drink one evening when Hendrik has gone to the country town, their gratitude takes on a peculiarly sympathetic tone since they know that she, poor woman, would like so much to share in the fun. But then, she is the wife of Hendrik. She has been married to a fortune, old and inherited, on which Hendrik's good or bad management has not been able to make much impression one way or the other, as yet at any rate. And in spite of all, the man is not so bad as he might be; at all events he has never said an angry word to his wife, so she ought to be pretty well off, folks think. That's so, Mariane admits; and she knows something else which the others can't see — that at bottom Hendrik is better, more upright, and more scrupulous than most farmers in the parish. And yet he torments and wearies her to death. The spoilt darling of peasant romance, the silent, lonely, stiff, proud peasant — Marie Bregendahl knows the kind, thoroughly and realistically, and her sympathy with these stiff, reserved natures takes the form of compassion, for those who *are like that,* and for those who have to live with them. And at times she smiles at them, very quietly.

Hendrik i Bakken is reserved, silent, and cross, partly because he is so frightfully ugly and knows it. So he throws up a rampart around himself, of irritating habits and unpleasant manners and an intolerably cantankerous bearing. He does stupid things out of pure cussedness; in the same spirit he behaves curiously, even scandalously, above all after losing his wife. People are not to see that he mourns her. For he has so many things to mourn for, more bitter and grievous than the loss of Mariane. He pads about his fields at night and in the mist, and with him goes one of his little boys, the one who has inherited his father's unhappy nature. " Ah, your mother, Ole, *she* could be merry too. — And she'd have liked to be fond of *me.* Ay, she'd have *liked* to be that! But she *couldn't!* " he said in a half-stifled voice.

It was eight years before Marie Bregendahl published another book, but then it was a masterpiece. *En Dödsnat* [1] is overpowering, thrilling; a swarm of people throngs its pages, and every single figure is intensely alive. Technically the little book is an almost faultless work of art, so surely has Fru Bregendahl mastered her subject, so unsentimentally does she arrive at the highest

[1] *A Night of Death,* English translation by Margery Blanchard (New York: Alfred A. Knopf; 1931) .

pathos. The narrative covers a space of about twelve hours. A farmer's wife, Anne Gram of Broholm, is about to have her ninth child. She sits in the afternoon cutting sandwiches for her harvesters; on this day she is not equal to standing over the work in the larder as usual. The children come in, and this change, seeing their mother cutting bread and butter in the dining-room, is enough to make them jubilant. The warm summer afternoon, with her whole flock swarming about Anne for the last time, acquires a strange radiance, like a sunset under the edge of storm-clouds. — Soon after, the children are told to go off to their grandmother's and stay there till sent for. Then the grown-ups forget the children entirely, as they realize that the confinement will be a hard one and that Anne Gram's life is at stake. Left alone, the children have to find out for themselves what is happening at home. The bigger girls, of eleven or twelve, have been through the same thing several times, they know enough to be frightened and anxious. The smaller ones guess something; the smallest of all simply have a grand time in their grandmother's empty rooms, happily ignorant of the misfortune threatening them. Two little cousins drop in by chance to visit the grandmother. And the four girls, the two eldest from Broholm and their cousins from Vældbjerg, together go through the turmoil of emotions of this night of death — terror and hope, impotent ignorance and light-minded forgetfulness, since it is humanly impossible to endure pain and anxiety for long at a time; they have to steal a little relaxation now and again. All that the grown-ups are going through is shared by the children, only more intensely — the helplessness, the hopes on the arrival of the doctor, the pent-up talkativeness which collapses in hopeless resignation, after the old doctor has given up. In the grey dawn a score of people, grown-ups and children, steal out of the bedroom where Anne Gram lies white and drained of blood. A mother is dead, the pillar that sustained a whole microcosm has been shattered, a little community has suffered irreparable loss. Never has womanly power and a woman's might been described as in this book. And the chilling desolation this gentle, artless woman leaves behind in her kingdom makes one shudder.

Marie Bregendahl is an unrivalled child-psychologist. Above all in our day, when one constantly meets with stories of children, often good in their way, but dressed up as it were, as though the author consciously or unconsciously had adapted his memories or his knowledge of children in agreement with a model or a recipe, Marie Bregendahl's child figures strike one as astonishingly real and alive. She certainly does not draw from the model; her studies are done in the open air and from the life. Under the title *Med aabne Sind (With Open Mind)* she has collected a group of stories about the two little girls from the Vældbjerg farm, Elsbeth and Grethe. With open mind — impressions shower down upon them day in, day out, throughout their childhood, scenes and sensations; games and fanciful conceits that spring from obscure sources in their own childish minds astonish themselves so much that the memory of them persists like the memory of incomprehensible and unforgettable events. They catch something essential or unessential of what goes on in the grown-up world, hear or ignore what their elders say to them, and snap up fragments of conversations which were not intended for their ears. A great deal of it runs off them like water off a duck's back — there is *some* truth in the myth of bygone generations about childhood's freedom from care and in the old sayings: " Children's tears are soon dried," " A child is easily pleased." It *is* incredible what children can forget and how quickly a child's sorrow may be dissolved into nothing, as it were. But it is equally true that children can undergo an experience in such a way that it is *never* forgotten, and this may happen while the child is surrounded by grown-up people who have no idea of what is going on in the child's mind, or even that anything *is* going on. Impressions sink deep into the open mind, inflicting on it wounds which never heal, or leaving scars for a lifetime. Or a joy, the cause of which even the child itself cannot remember, grows into a memory of golden light shed upon a piece of its childhood's world and of the sappy scent which life exhaled when it was young.

And sometimes it is hard to understand why a catastrophe should glance off the little pachyderm without leaving a trace, while an apparently insignificant event may give rise to disturbances in the childish mind and complexes inimical to life. The child's state of health is a contributing factor — its constitution as well as its condition at the moment. A deficiency of organic well-being is responsible for inferiority complexes at least as dangerous as those brought about by deprivation due to circumstances. A child suffering from intestinal sluggishness stores up memories of disappointments and misunderstandings which would scarcely be noticed by a youngster with the digestion of an ostrich. It is also true that children and grown-ups do not regard the same events as essential. And besides — what the majority of grown-ups are most likely to notice in children is their common peculiarities. They usually fail to see that the difference between one person and another, between divergent types of mind, is in reality more sharply expressed in childhood than in later life. The terrible thing about all theories of child-psychology is that when teachers and parents with no ear for human peculiarities have to practise academic theories upon living youngsters, they always apply the right rules to the wrong children.

Elsbeth and Grethe have been sent on a visit to a friend of their mother's. They have a fine time on the strange farm, but the best of all is a little herd-boy who is extraordinarily kind to them and clever at finding things to amuse them. One day this boy is accused of having stolen some score of eggs which were lying in a basket in the barn. The farmer and his wife treat him with horrible cruelty and spitefulness; with beating and threats they try to force a confession out of the boy, and finally he is turned away from the farm. The two little sisters stand and watch their friend being ill-treated and abused — and not a word do they say. And then it was they who had taken the eggs — or rather they hadn't taken them at all, they merely emptied them out in the hay and took the basket to use in their play-room. What keeps them from speaking is such a lot of things, they can't really make head or tail of it themselves — all the ugly words about thieving and rascality frighten them, the furious farmer and his wife are strangers, they have a vague feeling that nobody would understand if they tried to explain what they were about; they are at the same time afraid and bashful and uncertain. When things have calmed down after the storm, Elsbeth goes and buries the eggs in a patch of mud. To her the memory of their friend who suffered wrong and of their own cowardice becomes a mental sore — it galls and sears her even when she is an old woman. When she reminds Grethe of the incident it appears that her sister has only a very faint recollection of it: ah yes, there was something about some eggs, wasn't there, that the woman at Lide had lost?

" They are so terribly rare, those moments in life when all one's thoughts and feelings are wholly free to centre on the same thing," says Wise Sine, the old maid at Broholm who is given to talking like a book. The realist Marie Bregendahl is certain that this is as it should be. By Anne Gram's death-bed stand her two eldest daughters — Helga, the headstrong girl who has shown herself curiously unfeeling during all the harrowing ups and downs of the night, does not shed a tear even now, but she is pale as a corpse. The more easily moved Lise is dissolved in tears. But then the old doctor, who has seated himself on the night-stool by the bed, makes a sudden movement, and the pot inside the antiquated commode begins to roll about, making a sound just like a game of skittles, and Lise cannot help smiling through her tears. It appears too that in later life the stubborn Helga succumbs to the blows of misfortune, breaking like hard but brittle cast iron. Lise shows far more endurance, because her mind can find room for a variety of feelings at the same time, her thoughts can range about and take a respite among cheerful everyday things, even in the darkest hours. No — God help those who are like Hendrik i Bakken and his little son Ole: " When I think, it's only the one thing I think about."

Marie Bregendahl *is* of peasant birth, knows life as it shaped itself in farm and cottage — she certainly feels no temptation to romanticize the grim and silent men and women, the hard and crabbed natures. The softer kind who can bend beneath misfortunes and sorrows as living plants rooted in deep soil bend under the storm but straighten themselves again, glistening when sunshine returns — these are her favourites. She admires the way they get over their difficulties, and in the old, narrowly confined peasant community it is these brighter and gentler people who are able to help their neighbour in a bad hour and spread some of their cheerfulness in good times. None of Fru Bregendahl's heroines has been offered to the reader's admiration and amusement with so much wit and tenderness as *Hanne ved Höjen* (Hanne of the Knoll), the little old peasant woman whom life has tried so sorely without in the smallest degree lessening her love of life and her benevolent interest in her neighbour.

Hanne has a granddaughter who is also called Hanne and is married to a cattle-buyer in Hamburg. The marriage turns out worse than badly. And one day Hanne runs away from Hamburg home to her old grandmother to die. Not that she means this quite literally. But she is so mortally weary of living. And Hanne thinks that nowhere will she have such a sense of mortality, of the evanescence of all things, of the coffin-lid being slammed down sooner or later on all that lives, as with the old woman. For Hanne of the Knoll is now nearly eighty; she may well be ready to follow all those she has seen die before her.

Hanne lost her first husband when she was thirty; she was left a widow with six little children. To be sure, her husband was much older than Hanne, five-and-twenty years older, to be precise; he was rather queer in many ways, and of a gloomy nature. But what of that? — it was he who left her the fine farm that was now hers, she learned so much of him, oh yes, she was fond enough of her first husband, she mourned him and missed him. But when she had been a widow three or four years, Thomas came along. He was so handsome, and he was the same age as herself, and so it was a pair of them. And she came to understand what it meant to have a real sweetheart — positively a youthful sweetheart. But unhappily Thomas had a weak chest. After a few years of happy married life Hanne had to say goodbye to him too. But lastly Thorvald came — the most remarkable happening in Hanne's life. The daughters of her first marriage were already grown up; they didn't quite like Hanne's wanting to marry Thorvald. If their mother had even looked about for a suitable match, some middle-aged widower or other — since she had taken it into her head to change her state again. But Thorvald — Thorvald was a sort of bookish person, a surveyor, only twenty-nine. This was the great springtime of Hanne's life — the old woman subsided into smiles and dreams whenever she spoke of her third husband. But she was not allowed to keep him either — the romance lasted a bare nine months. And the child Thorvald left her with, the love-child, well, that boy never came to much; he was as kind as could be and so good, but somehow he couldn't make anything go. And there was her daughter, Anne of Broholm, who died and left all those little children — ay, death and sorrow had visited old Hanne and made havoc among her nearest and dearest. But as for being her intimates — no, she had never let them be that. Often as they had invaded the farm on the knoll, they had never been allowed to stay there for good.

And the younger, life-weary Hanne walks in and is clasped in the arms of a smiling and weeping grandmother — a grandmother whose exuberant and affectionate interest encircles her visitor and overflows in little outbursts of enthusiasm over the fine coat from Hamburg and her granddaughter's veil and parasol — bless me, is that what they wear now out in the great world? Hanne's mind is able to embrace a whole multitude of cheerful little things at the same time, like a flowery frame surrounding life's great joys and sorrows. Hanne from Hamburg discovers that weariness of life and gloomy thoughts die a natural death in her grandmother's company. She is standing in the privy one day — a little room which old Hanne has arranged with all imaginable rustic comfort and charm; outside the window the old woman is joking with some children who have been enticed into the yard by the smell of the cakes Hanne is baking. The younger Hanne wistfully moves a little vase of red auriculas which someone has stood on the window-sill, as a decoration for this place of solitude and peaceful meditation. And she discovers that she is alive, and that life is good, at this moment at any rate.

The little tale of Hanne of the Knoll ends with the preparations for Hanne's annual visit to the graves of her three husbands. Chance has willed that they shall all lie buried a long way from her home, and in three different churchyards. Three of Hanne's prettiest pot-plants are selected, the pots scrubbed, and the plants tidied up. And as the drive is going to take the whole day, why not invite as many of the girls of the neighbourhood as the carriage can hold — and as it *is* to be an excursion, then why not hire the innkeeper's big charabanc and take some more? The innkeeper's wife at Lilholm, where Thomas is buried, makes a lovely fricassee of mutton, so that's the place for dinner, and at Fjordby, where Thorvald lies, you can get good coffee. Cakes and raspberry liqueur must be brought from home in a basket. And the guests, who have tactfully presented themselves in a kind of half-mourning for the occasion, are ordered to change into bright and cheerful summer frocks — and Hanne from Hamburg must take both her red veil and her red parasol. Gay and radiant with flowers and pretty girls, the charabanc bowls along in the sunshine with old Hanne on her summer visit to the dead.

Marie Bregendahl's humour, when she is at her best, is very charming. She has full command of the old rustic art of story-telling which can tell a tale in such a quietly innocent way that the hearer can never be sure whether the story-teller himself sees the fun of it — till the point shoots out, bright and laughing. Then there is no more — or perhaps as an anticlimax a few little neutral sentences which seem to lock up the joke in a drawer, to be kept till one needs something amusing to think about. " *Opsvinget* " (" The Stroke of Luck ") , in Fru Bregendahl's last book of short stories, *Möllen (The Mill),* is a very charming example of this side of her talent.

Under the title *Södalsfolket (The People of Södal)*
she has recently collected in two volumes a number of
her stories of life in the little district of North Jutland
which is the scene of most of her writings. She does not
disguise the fact that her affection and her interest are
chiefly concerned with the old Södal people and with
the life of the district at the time when every farm was
still an independent microcosm and the village a cir-
cumscribed community — that is, the time when agri-
culture had not yet been industrialized and the farmers
had not been urbanized.

The same people pass in and out of each other's stories
— Christense, the widow at the mill, with her eleven
tall sons and one daughter, the crook-backed Jörgen
Damgaard, doleful and sagacious, Hanne of the Knoll
and the swarm of her descendants and relatives, Peter
Golddigger, who plants trees on the moorland — and
then all the young ones, sons and daughters at the farms,
servants and hangers-on. In the periphery of the Södal
people's life move the persons of quality, the squire of
Holmegaard and his daughter, Dr. Lund of Fjordby, the
Dean, amiable and authoritative and highly respected by
his congregation, whom he leads with great skill on a
middle course between official Christianity and conservative peasant paganism. The Church plays a certain part
in the life of the Södal people, as a centre for the more
solemn emotions, as the place where life's fateful moments — a child's incorporation in the family, the children's admission to the grown-up world, marriage, and

death — receive consecration; besides which it is at
church that the people of the widely scattered farms and
lonely crofts meet one another, hear and discuss news.
But religion plays no very important part, beyond that
of all religions in a peasant community, where people
feel their dependence on powers they cannot trust to
incline according to their wishes. To the children Christian doctrine is mainly a source of brooding over in-
soluble riddles and of anxiety. During their hard-work-
ing years of maturity the thought of such things slips into
the background. Only when folks are so old that their
toothless gums find it hard to chew and their weary
bodies fail under the stress of daily work does the longing or hope of a good rest " in God's bright mansions "
awake within them.

Marie Bregendahl's Södal stories do not paint the old
peasant life in any rosy colours exactly. Her people torment and cheat one another, misjudge and ridicule and
misunderstand their neighbours; gossip is rife and ven-
omous. But in looking back it is rightly the good people,
those who made life easier for the others, those who understood and could afford to make friends and keep
them, who are the great and dominating figures in the
landscape. And words of wisdom and sound sense seem
doubly strong when they rise above an ocean of chatter
and nonsense and trivial talk. We see Marie Bregendahl's Södal as it first appeared to the eyes of the child —
as Elsbeth and Grethe saw it when they went to visit
their grandmother in the little house under the shade

of the Broholm garden. From the top of the hill they have to cross, the country lies before them like an open book of fairy-tales, full of strange pictures. For instance, there is a long white house on another hill — with a big clump of trees at one end and a little outhouse for a head, the girls think the farm looks like a baby in swaddling-clothes. The smithy becomes a troll with flaming mouth, a house at the foot of an ancient barrow they call Birthe the cake-woman under her big umbrella. There is no end to all the wonders the children get out of this view. There comes a day when their fairy-book is shut up with a bang — they witness the horrors of a burning farm, and after that neither the countryside nor life itself can show its old face again to the two children. But in the changing lights of weather and seasons the familiar landscape varies its expression like a living face, and the well-known landmarks seem to be in continual motion, altering their appearance in harmony with the moods of the people who confront their good or evil fortune with this scene before their eyes.

It is obvious that Marie Bregendahl possessed peculiar qualifications for writing the history of the Danish peasant community during the last two generations. She has done so in the four-volume novel about *Holger Hauge og hans Hustru* (Holger Hauge and His Wife). If the book has become the monumental work it is, looming so proudly in recent Danish literature, it is due to Fru Bregendahl's description of this couple, the peasant-born

Lieutenant Hauge who returns to the land and becomes an agriculturist, and Kirstine Vendelbo, granddaughter of the soçager who had to cripple himself riding the timber mare; Kirstine with the powerful instinct of bettering herself, not by climbing out of the peasant class, but within it, as a peasant woman who has her class at heart. She herself has no idea of being a pioneer in the advance of her class towards economic independence and political power. She claims no knowledge beyond that of domestic affairs. True, she is a skilled dairywoman, but that is merely because she was left a widow on the death of her drunken first husband, alone with two little children to support. But when Holger Hauge marries her she becomes the driving force behind his numerous undertakings, the soil which enables the young officer from the town to take root on his own farm. She has the common sense, the tact, which the newcomers need to gain acceptance in the neighbourhood, the solidarity with all that is best in the old peasant culture. Hauge has energy, initiative; his restless mind is receptive of modern ideas, inquisitive, and hungry to experiment and discover chances of fresh enterprises. But without Kirstine he is nevertheless doomed to failure. He is like the mill; Kirstine is the one who fills it with corn; when she dies he runs empty. Realizing this, in the first days of their acquaintance she parries his amorous advances, suppresses her own longing to give herself to the man — instinctively she knows that only in marriage can she continue to be to him what Holger Hauge will never cease to need — a strong and faithful embrace in which night after night he can find release from the tension and feverish unrest of body and mind, so that he may wake up rested and refreshed, a helpmate who day after day saves her querulous husband work and annoyance, smooths out difficulties, encourages him, gives good advice without caring whether it is received ungraciously so long as it is followed — as it usually is.

Superficially viewed, their married life is not particularly harmonious or happy. He is egocentric, an essentially contentious nature, reacting violently to thwarting emotions, but taking prosperity and favourable events as merely his natural right. He is neither very chivalrous nor kind to his wife. By no means bad to his stepchildren, but thoughtlessly egoistic in his relations with them — they are Kirstine's alone, it is her business to do what is necessary for them. And he does not get on too well with his neighbours — it makes him arrogant and challenging when he meets with opposition to his plans, excellent in themselves, for co-operation in the exploitation of their new opportunities, on the part of conservative old farmers and crafty ones who would rather forgo increased profits than see Hauge make more money too. Kirstine's life is neither easy nor amusing — but it is profoundly satisfying. For she knows all the time, and Hauge knows now and then, that, after all, their life is a rich one because they share it. Occasionally, some night or some day, they are both aware of coming upon a treasure which is theirs in common; a priceless thing, which ordinarily lies concealed beneath worries great and small and tiresome routine, comes to light and gives them a spell of radiance and warmth.

The long novel which tells of the life of this couple during a period full of events and changes in the intellectual life of Denmark and in the structure of Danish society naturally contains much which is not quite so interesting to foreigners as to Danes. And around the persons of Holger and Kirstine there circulates a swarm of people, the whole rustic community of farmers, labourers, and gentry. Fru Bregendahl has not succeeded in making all these figures equally alive and convincing; but the drawing of the two chief characters is a signal triumph for her art.

Kirstine remembered her own grandfather, who belonged to the days before the peasants' emancipation, and she herself lived through a quarter-century's development of the Danish peasant class: the victory of the co-operative movement, the " change of system " in Danish politics, the government of the Left, the farmer and the parish clerk in ministerial posts. And she saw the farm workers, the day labourers, organize themselves in order to protect their interests — below the emancipated peasant class new strata had formed among the oppressed and powerless who wished to rise. — Doubtless it will always be so — such strata will always tend to form below any social class which has reached the surface and has a chance of giving its inherent qualities more or less free play.

At the age of fifty Kirstine Hauge is worn out; her
health is broken by an abdominal complaint and during
the long months in hospital her mind is tortured by
anxiety: Holger and she were the same age when they
came together; now she is old, an invalid, and he is
still a man in his prime, handsome, full of vitality, and
attractive to women. She is a prey to crises of jealousy,
weariness of life, intense bitterness, but a whole life's
self-discipline does not fail her: while devoured within
by pain and impatience, she is the helpful, sympathetic,
kind, and constant friend of her fellow-sufferers in the
hospital. And then she is allowed to come home — and
in her last hours she sees her life as it was, an abundant,
fruitful life in giving and receiving affection. She is
what her husband has made her, and he is transformed
by her; and around them is the farm which together
they have wrested from neglected fields and wastes of
heather, their children, their garden, their animals.
When she has looked upon all this for the last time, she
dies.

So Holger Hauge has to carry on; he is still full of
energy and initiative, but now it is all bustle and restless-
ness; the mill works on, empty of corn. He can't have
done with the female sex either, for a long time yet —
gets mixed up in some fairly humiliating and ridiculous
affairs. He does not fit into the new age, the post-war
period, and he doesn't like it. Is it merely that he has
grown too old — or is he right in regretting what was lost
when the course of events led to man's and woman's

share in work and in civilization becoming interchange-able? Had human development reached its most valu-able, most profoundly culture-promoting phase when man and woman each took possession of their own spheres in life, tried to perfect themselves in their re-spective fields, so that when they could meet and com-bine the results they had attained, they could say with old Hauge: " A man is a man, a woman is a woman, but a human being — *a human being,* Rördam, that is a man *and* a woman."

To sum up, it may be said that Marie Bregendahl's whole work is a monument to this human being who was two individuals in one, a man and a woman, to the few complete ones who were able to reach this state, and to the many human moieties and embryonic ones who were not fortunate enough to realize themselves in such a whole.

(1937)

MARGERY KEMPE OF LYNN

THE SPECTACLE of the wife of an English burgess writing her memoirs must have been a rare one in the fifteenth century. Of course it is a fact that throughout the Middle Ages a vast number of women wrote books, with their own hand or with the aid of a secretary. The only strange thing is the extent to which people have forgotten, since the Reformation and outside the Catholic tradition of culture, that in the whole of Catholic western Europe no one ever thought it more " unwomanly " to write books than to bake bread. On the contrary, it was nowhere considered unseemly for women to follow learned occupations and busy themselves with pen and ink, whereas in many parts, in Vorarlberg and Switzerland for instance, it was inadmissible for women to milk cows or tend cattle. These things were — and are still to some extent — men's work in those countries. Moreover, in the opinion of some anthropologists, such was the case in all primitive pastoral cultures.

Most mediæval women's books, however, come under the head of religious literature. Many of them have become Catholic classics and are read to this day, not only by the learned. Extracts from the writings of Gertrudis and Mechtildis are still current as books of edification, and within the Dominican Order the influence of Catherine of Siena is still exceedingly great. But there have always been exceptions. Roswitha of Gandersheim, a Saxon nun who lived in the ninth century, wrote historical epics and Latin dramas. In the twelfth century St. Hildegard of Bingen wrote her views on the natural philosophy of her time and other philosophical treatises. Marie de France, who lived in England about the time of Snorre Sturlason, composed fashionable tales in verse. We may well call Marie a moralizing author, but it was not Christian morals that she was concerned with — she preached the claims of love to the pretty young wives of tiresome husbands and the virtue of discretion to their lovers. Her *Lais* were translated into the Norse tongue in the time of Haakon Haakonsson, but whether they contributed to the corruption of morals in Old Norway I cannot offer an opinion.

But Margery Kempe's book is something unique in the literature of the Middle Ages. Fragments of it have long been known, but it was believed that the work in its entirety, *The Book of Margery Kempe,* was lost, and it was assumed that it was a book of religious meditations, written by an anchorite, which is what her first editor calls her. And in fact the fragments of Margery's writing that were printed by Wynkyn de Worde and afterwards reprinted many times — most recently by Professor Edward Gardner in *The Cell of Self-Knowledge* — pointed to Margery's having been a contemplative mystic of the English school, whose greatest name is Lady Juliana of Norwich. They bear witness to her power of finding pregnant expression for intense religious feeling: " Lord, because of Thy great pain, have mercy on my little pain." " When she saw the crucifix, or if she saw a man with a wound, or a beast, whichever it were, or if a man beat a child before her, or smote a horse or other beast with a whip, if she saw it or heard it, she thought she saw Our Lord being beaten or wounded, just as she saw it in the man or the beast." " Our Lord said to her: In anything thou dost, daughter, thou mayest no better please God than by believing that He loveth thee; for if it were possible that I might weep with thee, I would weep with thee, daughter, for the compassion that I have of thee." These are some of the sayings of Margery that were known.

Then it turned out that a manuscript of Margery Kempe's book had been lying all the time unnoticed in the library of Pleasington Old Hall, Lancashire. The present owner, Lieutenant-Colonel Butler-Bowdon, had discovered the old book even in his boyhood and had wondered what might be in it. So in 1935 he took it to an expert who identified the manuscript. An edition of the text furnished with the necessary learned apparatus will in due course be published by the Early English

Text Society. Meanwhile Colonel Butler-Bowdon has already issued his own translation — or transcription — in modern English. How the manuscript came to be in Pleasington Hall can only be a matter of conjecture. It originally belonged to the Carthusian monastery of Mount Grace, and it is not unlikely that when the monks were driven out by the creatures of Henry VIII they entrusted the contemporary Butler of Pleasington with some of their books and valuables to be preserved in the hope of better times. The Butlers are one of the old English families who have clung to their Catholic faith through all persecutions and adversity.

The world of English books, rich as it is, has thus been made richer by a unique work, and the mystical anchorite Margery Kempe reveals herself as anything but an anchorite, and a very original lady. It is true that many mediæval women's books occasionally give us biographical facts about their author and contain sections which throw light on the intimate and private daily life of their time. But, as has been said, most of them are purely religious works, and the most important of them were written by authors who were also saints. They write to proclaim God's love of human souls and to point out the ways by which He leads souls to increasingly intimate union with Him. Naturally a Gertrudis or a Birgitta or a Mechtildis has drawn on her own experience in this matter. But to them the main point is not that these things took place in *their* soul — it is that God's love expresses itself in the way they have known.

With the saint's absence of egoism they are entirely occupied with God's workings, and they are interested in
their own soul because it is the Deity's field of activity,
where He acts as they know He would gladly act in all
souls, if only they would allow Him.

But Margery Kempe was no saint — in any case she
did not become one in those years of her life of which
the memoirs give us an account. She fought bravely
against her sins and frailties, so far as she was aware of
them herself. But if other people — her confessors, for
instance — held a different opinion about anything in
her conduct, Margery was extremely unwilling to admit
that she did not know better herself. Her piety is absolutely sincere, she loves her Saviour ardently and intensely, and she really wishes to be allowed to suffer for
Him — scorn and disgrace and unpopularity in the
world, both because this was the lot of Christ and because she thinks she has deserved it on account of her
sins. But she would prefer to be persecuted and derided
for uttering God's word in and out of season, and because the children of this world are offended by the gifts
of grace she believes herself to have received — her visions and the violent and sensational forms assumed by
her religious ecstasies. But when people's displeasure
is expressed in mere commonplace gossip and flippant
talk, she does not like it at all. At the end of her book
she tells us that during a stay in London she was recog-
nized by some people who met her in the street — Margery Kempe had by that time become a notorious and

controversial figure in England. In passing they said loud enough for her to hear: " Ah! thou false flesh, thou shalt no good meat eat." Margery is furious and explains in some detail what was referred to — a malicious fabrication which people had made up about her just after she had been converted. She was supposed to have been at table in the house of a well-to-do family; it was a fast day and red herring was served as well as fresh fish; there were some boiled pike which were perfectly delicious. Margery was said to have let the dish of herring go past her: " Ah! thou false flesh, thou wouldst now eat red herring, but thou shalt not have thy will." Whereupon she helped herself to the pike. This story must have been at least twenty years old when Margery was reminded of it in London, but she refutes it as energetically as ever and attributes its invention to the Devil himself.

But it is precisely this self-absorption of Margery's that we may thank for the extraordinarily intimate and lively descriptions of people and circumstances to be found in her reminiscences. The old Eve, restless and self-assured and opinionated, dies hard in her, and she reacts violently to everything that befalls her. She gives us a variety of information about life in Lynn, and goes on to tell us about her experiences on her endless pilgrimages, at first all over England, and then by land and sea across the whole of Europe and as far as the Holy Land. We even have a little glimpse of Norway. On her last voyage, when she accompanied her son's widow, who was returning to Danzig, their ship was forced to shelter at some place on the Norwegian coast — unfortunately she does not tell us where. But the travellers went ashore on Good Friday and stayed till Easter Monday. We are told that " after the custom of the country, the Cross was raised on Easter Day about noontime," so that Margery could have her devotion before it with weeping and sobbing as well as if she had been at home. On the Monday before they sailed, all on board received the body of the Lord, which must have been brought to them by the local Norwegian priest. As mediæval Church custom demanded that confession should immediately precede the reception of the Sacrament of the altar, we may suppose that the Norwegian priests along the southern trade routes must have had some knowledge of the lingo of the Baltic seafarers.

Margery was born about 1373 at King's Lynn, Norfolk. This town was at that time one of the most important markets in England, and Margery's family belonged to the circle of the leading burgesses in the place. At the age of twenty she was married to a young man, John Kempe, who was regarded as a suitable match. There were fourteen children of the marriage, who play a surprisingly small part in her reminiscences. She only refers directly to one son. His mother wished that he should shun the sins and wickedness of the world and follow Christ, but all she gained by it was that her son shunned his mother and her godly exhortations. He went to sea and finally settled down at Danzig as a trader. There he fell ill, after a fairly wild bachelor life. He himself and everyone else thought it was leprosy. So when he came home to Lynn he was repentant and begged his mother's forgiveness and her intercessions. Margery prayed and did penance for her son, and he recovered and returned to Danzig and his trading. He married a German girl. Her other children are only referred to in one passage, where she gives an account of her usual observance of prayer. First she always prayed for the spiritual welfare of all on earth, and then it was her custom specially to mention " all my children, ghostly and bodily, that Thou make their sins to me by true contrition, as it were mine own sins, and forgive them as I would that Thou forgive me."

She was dangerously ill after the birth of her first child and sent for her confessor. There was a sin which she had never been able to bring herself to confess, and even now she found it hard to speak of it. The priest was somewhat severe with her, and exhausted as the young wife was, spiritually and physically, this had the effect of disturbing her mind. For eight months she was tormented with diabolical visions and temptations to suicide, she raged and scoffed and was as spiteful to her husband as she could be. But one evening she had a vision: Jesus Himself came and sat down on the edge of her bed. He looked at her so gently and tenderly that she began to take heart. Then He said: " Daughter, why hast thou forsaken Me, and I forsook never thee? "

Now she must have felt that she ought to be grateful

to God and show it by serving Him. But she was proud
and vain and took no serious step to reform herself. She
dressed in a way that made her the talk of the whole
town, and she could not bear other women having finer
clothes or more precious jewels than herself. Her craving for admiration was insatiable. When her husband
mildly asked her to be a little less provocative in her
bearing, she replied curtly and irritably that he ought
never to have married her — her father had been mayor
and the biggest man in town, and she was going to act
up to her birth.

In order to be financially independent of her husband
she started a brewery, and in a year or two Margery was
one of the biggest brewers in the town. But then things
went badly and she lost a lot of money over it. Again
she tried her hand in industry — this time a horse-mill
and a bakery. But this too turned out badly. The neighbours were delighted. But Margery began to think that
perhaps Our Lord wished to cure her of her love of gain.
And one night, as she lay beside her husband, she heard
" a sound of melody so sweet and delectable that she
thought she had been in Paradise." And she lamented:
" Alas, that ever I did sin! It is full merry in Heaven."

But neighbours and friends had a hearty laugh when
the worldly Margery Kempe took to discoursing about
God and heaven. And she, who till now had insisted on
full sensual satisfaction in her conjugal life, was seized
with an equally violent longing to be freed from her
wifely duties. She besought her John that they might

both make a vow of chastity. (According to Catholic doctrine, which maintains the indissolubility of marriage, it is not permissible for one of the partners to make this vow unless the other is willing to do the same.) For the time being, John Kempe was altogether opposed to promising anything of the sort. For all these years he had been a good, affectionate and very patient spouse, and it was natural enough that for the present he should adopt a sceptical attitude towards his intractable wife's complete change of front. For now Margery thought of nothing but penance and fasting, neglected her household for daily and nightly devotions, and dragged the unfortunate John with her to church festivals and places of pilgrimage.

John was soon to be proved right in doubting Margery's transformation. For two years she carried on her exalted religious practices and showed abhorrence for cohabitation with her husband. And then all at once she was seized with an equally exalted passion for another man — one who had spoken to her a few times outside the church and made her dishonourable proposals, perhaps only in fun, to see how far Margery was in earnest in this new way of attracting attention to herself. But Margery fell headlong in love with the man — and came to the conclusion that God had cast her out, since He could let her be subjected to such a temptation. She gave up fighting against it, went to the man and offered herself. It turned out that he didn't want to have anything to do with her.

Margery went home, desperately humiliated and crushed. And when she thought upon her fall from grace she thought she must be driven mad with despair. For a long time her soul was tossed hither and thither between hopelessness and hope, remorse and rebellion, longing for true conversion and a life in God and temptations to fling herself into a wild life of sin, to go to ruin or take her own life. But one day as she knelt in church she had another vision: Jesus appeared to her again and spoke to her of His love for her soul. And all He asked was that she should return it. In His love she would find forgiveness for all her sinfulness. And if she would love Him in return, this love of hers would bring her so much persecution in this world that it would suffice for her penance.

Now there begins a new phase of Margery Kempe's life. Prayer and contemplation take the form of " visions " and long dialogues. With her " inner comprehension " she hears Jesus speaking to her, and she speaks to Him. Sometimes He brings His mother with Him, or various saints. These experiences can hardly have been actual visions. But Margery had pronounced literary talent, as her book bears witness, packed as it is with aptly narrated scenes and sketches of people she had met. And she had absorbed the narrative of the Gospels as one absorbs a thrilling novel. She identifies herself with every scene and follows the Saviour's life on earth as though she were a contemporary and belonged to His most intimate circle. She is with Mary at Bethlehem and

Nazareth, helping her in the nursery and the housework. She accompanies her and the apostles to Golgotha, and after the entombment she goes home with them to the house of John; she persuades Mary to lie down, while Margery goes into the kitchen and makes her a bowl of strong soup. But Mary refuses food, she will do nothing but mourn — until Peter knocks at the door, in such despair at his denial of the Lord that he needs consolation even more than she herself. Then Mary rises from her bed and goes out to him: " Ah! Peter, dread thee not, for, though thou hast forsaken my sweet Son, He forsook never thee," she comforts him. This is an echo of the same words that Margery herself thought she heard from the mouth of Jesus, when in her young days she had her first " vision." And when all is said and done, in a way Margery is right of course in saying that all good thoughts which occur to one are the voice of God speaking in our soul. Her love of Christ is perfectly sincere, and many of the imaginary conversations she carried on with Him are of great beauty and show deep religious insight. But it is probable that this interweaving of piety and poetical fancy was just what made Margery so naïvely unsuspicious of many of her own weaknesses — her preoccupation with self, her love of asserting herself, her unwillingness to take advice from others. She never succeeded in ridding herself of these, although her whole conscious ego was turned towards God and she lived only to pray and do penance and to preach Christ's love and God's glory.

To some extent she may indeed have had aural hallucinations, as when she heard celestial music. She was a pronounced psychopath — if by nothing else, this is proved by the violent revulsions of her mind, going from one extreme to another. And after her final conversion her religious emotion is expressed in sobbing and weeping. She herself counted this as a gift of grace, and of course she could quote a number of theological authorities for regarding tears of repentance as a gift of grace. But by degrees her fits of weeping took the form of violent attacks, whenever she approached the sacraments or thought intensely of Christ's life upon earth. She began to shriek wildly — she roared, as she says herself — and often collapsed in convulsions, causing the whole congregation to crowd about her. It is very natural that many priests could discover nothing edifying in such disturbances of divine service and firmly refused to believe that it was God who was responsible for Mistress Kempe's disorderly behaviour. And a great part of the congregation thought the woman was only trying to make herself interesting — she was shamming. Or perhaps she suffered from falling sickness.

These attacks of Margery's cannot, however, have been epileptic, for while they lasted she saw and heard everything that was said or went on around her, and she remembered it all clearly afterwards. And even after suffering from them for over twenty years, neither her bodily nor her mental powers were in the slightest degree impaired. She lived her life of religious vagabondage on constant pilgrimages, which must have been extremely fatiguing to an old person, when we consider what the roads and means of transport were like in her day. And all the time she is as receptive as ever to new impressions; she assimilates sermons and religious writings which are read aloud to her — above all, the books of the Bible, but also Walter Hilton's *Scala Perfectionis* and the English Carthusian mystics. Margery had once visited Lady Juliana of Norwich, whom she calls Dame Jelyan, and had stayed with her for several days, during which she accepted advice and guidance from the anchorite, who must at this time have been a very old woman. Margery was also acquainted with the writings of St. Bridget (of Sweden) and allowed herself to be influenced by them. She herself was unable to read, though she carried her prayer-book. But like so many women of the Middle Ages she probably managed to read a book the contents of which she knew pretty well by heart, which was not the same thing as spelling her way through works previously unknown to her. Her memoirs were dictated, at the age of something over sixty. All things considered, Margery Kempe was a gifted lady, a decidedly artistic nature, deeply religious and not a little hysterical.

Of course she carried her point and got John Kempe to release her from all the duties she owed him. Her account of her final settlement with her husband makes rather amusing reading. It took place on the highroad; they were on pilgrimage to York, and she carried the keg

of beer, while John had a loaf of bread in his bosom.
John Kempe was very unwilling to let her go, but her
prayers and fanaticism frightened him so that in the end
he had to give in. He showed sufficient practical sense
to insist that she should pay a share of their common
debts before releasing her and agreeing to her going her
own way. Jerusalem was Margery's first goal.

After quite a lot of adventures in England she got
away and had a number of remarkable experiences on
her way to and from the Holy Land. Margery's talent
as a narrator is at its very best in these descriptions of life
on the main pilgrim routes and of all the curious types
she met with among the crowds that frequented them.
We must suppose that they were all impelled by a more
or less conscious longing for the religious experience, as
well as by the belief that treasures were laid up where
neither moth nor rust could corrupt by going on a
pilgrimage, which was always a dangerous and somewhat
adventurous undertaking. But we must not forget that
the people of the Middle Ages knew no other form of
holiday travel and " tourism " than these pilgrimages.
And Margery had ample opportunities of learning that
by no means every pilgrim cared to be treated to evangelical tales and pious talk *all* the time while thus jour-
neying from one sanctuary to another. Time after time
her companions grew thoroughly sick of her and begged
her to leave them in peace and be merry and pleasant, at
least during mealtimes. Or else they made a start from
the inn during the night hours in order to get away from

her. So Margery was left behind and had to look for a new set of travelling companions — and when it came to the point these wouldn't have her either. There was the young English lady of noble birth who was travelling with a great retinue; at first she was delighted to have the company of the celebrated visionary — but then she came across somebody who criticized Margery and her vagaries, and so the lady backed out of all her promises and declined to be seen in the company of Mistress Kempe. And there was the hunchbacked English beggar, Richard, whom Margery met in Venice and hired as her attendant. After a while he, too, came to hear so many queer things about her that he would not show himself with her in the daytime. Margery was robbed, had to beg her way — then she met people who believed in her mission, were edified by her talking, and gave her generous alms. After which she gave away all she had received and met with fresh adventures. For it must not be thought that the eccentric old Englishwoman lacked adherents. The Franciscans of Jerusalem had made much of her and were anxious to hear about her revelations; they were quite willing to believe it was the Holy Spirit that moved her when she had convulsive fits of weeping and had to " roar " whenever she came to a spot where Jesus had passed and suffered. And in the cottages of humble folk by the roadside the old pilgrim woman was often received with touching Christian charity.

She had received permission to take the Sacrament of

the altar every Sunday — a thing which was not so common in the Middle Ages. But she knew no language but English, so it was often difficult for her to confess. This was then arranged for her by Our Lord through a few little miracles. In Rome He once summoned St. John the Evangelist so that she might confess to him. Margery said her *Confiteor,* and the apostle gave her absolution and preached a sermon to her — she heard everything he said just as plainly as with her bodily ears, she assures us. Another time she met in the Lateran Church a German priest who took charge of her, and although he did not know a word of English till then, he learned in the course of a fortnight to understand Margery well enough for her to confess to him; but when other English people spoke he did not understand a word. So this too was accounted a great marvel by Margery. — In common with many other pious but self-centred people she was very ready to take any strange thing that happened to her as a direct miracle.

It is evident that in the eyes of her contemporaries Margery was an irritatingly anomalous phenomenon. Had she been a nun, or had she withdrawn to the cell of an anchorite, she might have behaved as eccentrically as she pleased. But in fact she was the runaway wife of a burgess, who strayed all over the world and foretold coming events. She undoubtedly had the power of seeing through many of her fellow-creatures and was able to tell them of their secret sins and weaknesses. Many of them — especially priests who had something to conceal — took it well, confessed that what she said was true, and begged for her intercession, that they might have strength to break with their sin. But others, again of the clergy, were extremely angry. — And then she would dress herself entirely in white, and keep unnaturally strict fasts — until she was told by the voice of Jesus within her that this would do for the present and she might eat and drink like other people for a time and take meat and beer on all but fast-days. And she was always on the move, and wherever she came she set folks talking about her.

Time after time she was brought before the ecclesiastical courts in England by kind neighbours and the like. They declared that the woman was a dangerous heretic, the worst Lollard in the whole country, and said they would be delighted to fetch wood to burn her. Margery was then examined as to her faith and her doings by a whole series of prelates. Now, we have all heard so much about the victims of the Inquisition that we are apt to overlook the fact that the activities of the Inquisition consisted very largely in exonerating the victims of their neighbours' suspicions and vindictiveness and releasing them with a written declaration that they were to be spared further accusations. It appears from Margery's account of all these examinations that she always met with fair play and honest treatment, even if several of her judges did not disguise their opinion that she was a nuisance and personally an unbearable female. But they admit that her preaching is entirely orthodox and that her piety is certainly sincere and free from hypocrisy. Others feel edified by her words and ask her advice in matters of conscience. Abbots and bishops invite her to dine at their table, " making much of her " and spending the evening in pious conversation with Margery " until the stars appeared in the sky."

She was obliged by ill health to settle again for a few years in her native town, and the good people of Lynn had something to talk about. It turned out as she had heard it foretold by Our Lord: " And so shall I be worshipped on earth for thy love, daughter, for I will have the grace that I have shown to thee on earth, known to the world, so that people may wonder at My goodness." But also: " Thou shalt be eaten and gnawed by the people of the world as any rat gnaweth stockfish." She succeeded in dividing the clergy of the town and its neighbourhood into two camps — for and against Margery Kempe. The most famous preacher in Lynn was a Franciscan, who was also known for his exemplary life. He refused to believe in Margery's revelations, had no sympathy for her way of living, and finally forbade her to come to the church where he preached, if she could not stop shrieking and making scenes. Margery was afraid it might end in a catastrophe with this friar — he was a model, to be sure, but it sometimes happened that even models fell from grace. On the other hand a number of the young priests in particular seem to have taken her side. This was natural enough in itself; young men who looked back on the harsh years of privation

at the grammar school and the university and were faced
by a life of celibacy attached themselves to the inspired
old woman whom they called " Mother " and formed
a kind of elective family about her. It was in this circle
that she found the confessor who for a number of years
served also as her reader and secretary. The idea that
it was particularly the vow of celibacy that was sinned
against by the bad priests of the Middle Ages is not confirmed by Margery's book — and for that matter it is
seldom supported by contemporary documents other
than those which are obviously tendentious and aimed
precisely at the immorality which of course was found
within the Church as elsewhere. The priestly faults
that Margery most frequently and mercilessly scourges
happen to be her own pet sins — greed of power, arrogance, the desire of honours, and disobedience to su-
periors.

For many years Margery had not been living with her
husband. Then it happened one morning that John
Kempe fell downstairs in his house and nearly killed
himself. Naturally the neighbours said it was all his
wife's fault for running away from him, and that if John
Kempe died she ought to be hanged. However, he was
sewed up and patched together, but among other in-
juries he had fractured his skull and he remained an
invalid as long as he lived. Margery then took him in
and nursed him. He was imbecile and helpless as an
infant, so most of her time was spent in keeping him
clean — and her money went for fuel, for he had to be

kept warm and she used such quantities of hot water; evidently she was fairly poor now. The worst thing to her mind was that she had so little time for prayer and contemplation; she could not even go to church every day. But Christ told her in her soul that she was now serving Him best in nursing her sick husband. So she looked after John as faithfully and affectionately as if he had been Christ Himself.

About this time her son from Danzig came home on a visit and brought his German-born wife with him. He was greatly changed, so pious and serious that Margery could not thank God enough for it. And when, a short time after his return, he fell ill and died, his mother was easy in her mind and of good cheer: he had only come home to Lynn in order to go on to his true home, the land of the living.

John Kempe died not long after, and now Margery's German daughter-in-law wished to return to her family and to her little girl whom she had left behind in Danzig. Margery was to accompany her to Ipswich and see her on board. But when she was there she could not resist her love of travel, and much against her daughter-in-law's wish and the advice of her confessor she insisted on making the voyage to Germany. In one of her spiritual talks with Our Lord she was expressly commanded to go. And " if God be with us, who can be against us? " Moreover she found a priest to whom she submitted the matter and who gave her the advice she looked for.

After many adventures by sea and land she reached Danzig at last and parted from her daughter-in-law — to the evident delight of the latter. But Margery had heard about the Precious Blood at Wilsnack in Brandenburg. In that place three Hosts were preserved which were said to have bled. Margery secured a passage to Stralsund with an English merchant who promised to help her on her journey, but when they came ashore he was by no means desirous of keeping his promise and accompanying her to Wilsnack. But Margery was not one to give in. She did not know the language of the country, she was now over sixty — which in mediæval times was considered a great age — and in addition she was ill; nevertheless she took up her pilgrim's staff and shamed her countryman into going with her. He went in fear during the whole journey — fear of thieves, of bandits in the trackless bogs and forests through which they had to pass, and evidently of Margery too, who constantly had her spiritual talks with Our Lord and who shrieked and wept freely. Now and then the man would walk so fast that Margery was almost broken-winded trying to keep up with him. At last she stopped at a little inn by the roadside; she could not walk another step. Then she hired a conveyance, and so she reached Wilsnack, where she worshipped the blood of Christ with ardent devotion and loud sobbing.

She wished to return overland, as she was subject to seasickness and had little heart for life on board a ship, though, following Our Lord's advice, she always stayed

at the bottom of the vessel and kept her cloak over her
head so as not to see the waves. She travelled by way of
Aix-la-Chapelle, but her journey was attended by endless difficulties. She could get no one to accompany her,
could find no lodging, people were horrid to her, and
she had to avoid districts where war was raging. But
Margery got there. Between Aix-la-Chapelle and Calais
she had the company, off and on, of a party of wild young
men, and with them was a young monk who was given
to drink and no better than his companions. Margery
evidently had a good influence on him and they parted
as good friends. Then she got a passage to Dover and
proceeded to London. It was on this occasion that she
encountered the scoffers who reminded her of the old
red-herring story. But there were also many high-born
gentlemen and ladies in London who overwhelmed her
with kindness, and she went about the town bravely de-
nouncing the sins of its inhabitants — profane swearing,
lying, loose living, drink, and luxury in food and dress.

With her account of her return from this journey
Margery's autobiography comes to an end. In a final
chapter she explains her habitual course of prayer. Of
her last days and her death we know nothing.

In one place she calls herself " one of Our Lord's own
secretaries, to whom He has shown His love." But her
firm conviction that by means of her book she would
lead innumerable souls to Christ and contribute might-
ily to the spreading of God's kingdom on earth was not
realized, so far as we can tell. The Mount Grace manu-

script, which must have been copied from the original as soon as the latter was finished, seems to have been unique. What good she may have done during her long and tempestuous life no one, of course, can now say. But the rediscovered book presents us with an incomparable picture of life at the beginning of the fifteenth century, and the self-portrait of a woman whose nature was a curious compound — of piety and egoism, humility and pride, charity and hardness, talent and hysteria — but who preserved her incredible vitality even in old age.

(1938)

CAVALIER

(Dichtung und Wahrheit)

HENRY LONGAN STUART was of Irish birth and received a classical education. He had served in the Italian and in the British army. He tried his luck in America as a cowboy, a journalist, and a war correspondent. His translations of Italian and French literature have been highly praised. His friends describe him as courageous, generous, witty, alive to all contemporary movements, and deeply rooted in Catholic faith and doctrine, an aristocrat in appearance and instincts, a democrat by conviction — a younger brother of the poet-soldiers whom a couple of centuries of Catholic persecution in Ireland had scattered over half the world. He died in 1928.

His only novel, *Weeping Cross,* which appeared in 1908, was scarcely noticed by the majority of critics and public. To most non-Catholics it appeared puzzling and repellent: it deals with *sin.* But although in the given situation the sin of the leading figure in the book was almost inevitable, neither he nor the author finds any excuse in this; God's supernatural grace is here treated as just as realistic a reality as the erotic instinct and the longing for earthly happiness, treason against God is regarded as just as shameful as treason against one's country.

But the greater part of Stuart's co-religionists were also scandalized by the book. The Catholics of America have been infected by the puritanical system of suppression — which is entirely un-Catholic. The system, that is, which assumes that Christian virtues are best protected if we pretend to know nothing of the dangers that threaten them, or that in any case we ought not to assume that they can be threatened by temptations against which there is no help but the will to rely on supernatural grace.

Now, Stuart's book takes the form of an old Jesuit father's autobiography. And although in his description of external events — even the erotic situations — Father Fitzsimon is as cautious as any seventeenth-century priest would naturally be (of course he is nevertheless more outspoken than would have been thought proper in the early years of this century), he relates the inner history of his fall, the story of how the will to forsake God arose in him and grew and affected all his mental powers, overdeveloping some and obliterating others of his original traits — so thoroughly and unsparingly that *Weeping Cross* is harrowing and often painful reading. In this impressively frank confession the Catholic hero strips himself of everything heroic. In the eyes of the great reading public, which at the time the book was first published was somewhat sentimentally and optimistically inclined, ready to understand and pardon human sins, if not exactly the individual sinners, it might certainly appear that *Weeping Cross* gave support to the enemies of the Catholic Church in many of what they considered their most serious charges against the Church in general and the Jesuit Order in particular: namely, that its care of souls fosters over-scrupulousness and encourages sadistic self-torture and self-abasement, as well as deceit and self-deceit. Many Catholic readers of *Weeping Cross* had a positive feeling that here Stuart had been telling tales out of school about matters which Catholics ought to keep to themselves — that is, if they ever happened to come across such extreme conflicts of conscience.

For from a purely worldly point of view a host of reasons can be found for excusing and almost for exonerating Richard Fitzsimon. Some slight tampering with the narrative, a little suppression of the deepest and most secret disloyalties and turpitudes of his nature — and he might have paraded as the romantic and nobly unfortunate hero in a tale of Cromwell's infamous treatment of Catholic Ireland. Richard is the young son of an Irish landowner, brave, proud, handsome, highly cultivated; from the Jesuit college he has gone to the army, but during his whole military career — in the Thirty Years' War, with Prince Rupert's cavalry in England, against Cromwell's troops in Ireland — he has always been determined to return to the cloister if he comes through alive. And he will have nothing on his conscience which might make him more unworthy to present the holy Sacrament than his humanity itself makes him. He has shown intrepidity and foolhardiness in action, mercy and gentleness in the intervals of fighting, he has cared for the sick and shared all he possessed with the poor, he has preserved his chastity — and the virginity of his heart. God is his only love and Mary is mistress of his soul.

One winter day in 1652 he is put ashore in Boston. Through the kind offices of Sir Harry Vane the death sentence on the Royalist has been reduced to ten years' penal servitude in the Colonies. His home in Ireland has been burnt down, his brother has fallen, his mother has succumbed during the flight before Cromwell's troops, the family estates are confiscated, and his father has been executed. Poor as Lazarus, Richard Fitzsimon is handed over to the hard-shelled, Bible-thumping pioneer community, where everybody hates him blindly and instinctively — on account of his faith, because he is Irish, and because he is a gentleman through and through and no affected humility can alter his unmistakable breeding. To begin with they put him to scavenging work in the town and with malicious delight give him every opportunity of feeling what it is like to be half-dead with hunger and cold. Until he is fetched by the man who has bought him. Then he has a collar riveted about his neck with his master's initials on it, and Squire Fleming takes him off to his farm in Connecticut.

From the first this old Scottish colonel lets his slave feel how he regards the relations between them — they are both officers and gentlemen; Mr. Fitzsimon has fought on the losing side and is, for the time being, his prisoner. He is here to work — that is so. Fleming works himself, his farm is a clearing in the primeval forest; his daughter works indoors and in the yard, and doesn't know what it is to act the lady. Colonel Fleming himself will show Mr. Fitzsimon how to set about it; with tactful kindliness he tries to find some way in which the clumsy and unpractical Richard may be useful — while he himself is only fit for preaching and fighting, as his daughter, Mistress Agnes, says. Even when Fleming finds out that Richard is a Catholic, the Scotsman, who is quite fanatical in his hatred of Catholicism, does not try to wound the feelings of a captive and defenceless opponent.

Fleming's daughter, Agnes Bartlett, is a widow, a few years older than Richard. He was a little boy when he left his home, which is now wiped off the face of the earth. For the first time he becomes acquainted with a home where thrift and industry reign, and where it is pleasant to rest after a tiring day in the fields or in the forest. The great kitchen where pine logs blaze on the hearth is the centre of this home, and it is ruled by a bonny young woman, full of kindly care for the well-being of all, glib of tongue, bitingly sharp when she thinks anyone needs correcting, with a nature that changes rapidly from sparkling gaiety to distant coldness, without any reason known to her household.

Richard gets his share of both her good and her ill humour. Alike they fill him with surprise. With his inexperience of women it is not long before he is brooding over Mistress Agnes's nature night and day. Shortly before her death she confesses to him that she began to love him the very day he came into the house. But at first she evidently cannot account to herself for her inability to leave this Cavalier in peace, when he has been sent to help her in the kitchen. She must have him hanging about her — one day she coaxes him without any conscious intention except to make him feel at home; she is trying to make him happy. Next day he gets on her nerves — she can't make him out, thinks him odd — and she wounds and lashes him with her sharp tongue. And afterwards begs his pardon, receives his reproaches almost with humility, laughs when he returns a biting answer. For in his intercourse with his " mistress " Richard's Irish wit acquires a new keenness. She questions him: What did Prince Rupert look like? And what about himself — did he, too, wear his hair in long curls, did he, too, go about in a silk sash and a lace collar when he was an officer in the King's army? Then she was once more the trim housewife and he the awkward yardboy: " Roll up my sleeves — right up to the shoulder, you clown," she commands him, with her hands deep in the kneading-trough. He has been accustomed to move among scented beauties in low-necked gowns, and they have never made any impression on either his senses or his heart. Now the sight of Agnes's bare white arms against her woolsey dress makes him hot and giddy, there is such ease and swiftness in her movements as she works. The scent of her hair and her healthy warm body blends with the smell of fresh-baked bread and sweet milk, of the cedar-wood she scours and the hay they bring in together.

No sooner does he realize that to him Agnes is nothing short of a temptation than he snatches at the most obvious excuse for not fighting against it in full earnest: the desire that awakens within him involves nothing that is sinful in itself. It is contrary neither to the law of God nor to the order of nature that a man of thirty should be seized with the longing to possess a wife and a home. Can he do otherwise than think how happy it must be to live with this lovely, healthy, capable woman in just such a clearing as this, far within the forests of the New World — to see crops and cattle thriving under one's own hands, and children the fruit of their union? Only for him such dreams are forbidden — knowing as he does that God has other designs for him and that he might just as well dream of plucking down the moon out of the sky as of taking Agnes Bartlett to wife. His self-pity is aroused and spreads its poison in Richard's soul. Knowing from his own experience that the mystical communion with God renders a man invulnerable in his heart of hearts, happy in spite of fetters, poverty, and abasement in the eyes of men, he is inclined to expostulate with God: " Thou treatest me more harshly than any other." This is nothing new to him — while the inmost core of his soul was proof against humiliation, his vanity has been vulnerable enough to petty rascalities. He has noted it with a kind of smile — such is our human weakness. But now he is neither able nor willing to fight any longer against his vanity, his hot temper, and his touchiness. The inward pride of the soldier-monk crumbles and is washed away by the lover's sensitiveness as to the figure he cuts in his mistress's eyes. Before he is aware of it the day arrives when he sees that the love of God which caused his father to go to the scaffold as a bridegroom to his wedding, which in his own case was once stronger than the fear of death or of men, is not strong enough to keep him from Agnes, if he has a chance of getting her.

He indulges in dreams that after all it may be possible for them to be married. If he could escape to Europe he would certainly be given a command in the army of the French King. Or an unknown friend in England might procure his pardon and a settlement in Maryland, where there is religious liberty. Agnes laughs him to scorn. She is not one to follow a troop of mercenaries with the baggage-train and the wenches. And he is no use for clearing land in America. All she knows is that they love each other boundlessly; as to the future, they must not think of it; now is the time for them to take what happiness they can get. The present moment is theirs.

Her first husband's " love " has left scars on her body

and soul. He was a good match, but her sound girlish instinct bade her refuse him nevertheless. Then he bribed her coloured maids and they let him into her bed-chamber one night. After that she was not good enough for any other man; it was only with him she could hope for a home and affection and children. It turned out a hell. When the Indians captured her husband and tor-tured him for four days before he died, she began once more to believe in the justice of God. And the man who is now wooing her — Captain Gideon, Richard calls him — is evidently not unlike her first. — Richard can make nothing of this morality. Surely she was as pure as before, in spite of a man having outraged her; but that the scoundrel should be rewarded by the gift of his victim and her dowry instead of by death — ! Agnes silences him impatiently — he knows no more of the world than a kitten! He does not understand the sys-tem of ideas in which she has been brought up and against which she reacts in defiance, any more than she understands his scruples of conscience and the conflict within him: it is mere exaltation on his part to imagine he is denying God if he becomes her lover — since that is the only way they can be united.

Then their love-story takes its tragic course, in joy and pain, sweetness and bitterness. Squire Fleming sets out on a long journey, and Agnes makes all preparations for their lawless nuptial night the very evening her father leaves the house. But the same day a strange Indian comes secretly to Richard and brings him a letter. The

Jesuits of the mission in Canada have discovered what has become of their former pupil. He has only to fly with the Indian — away from perdition, home to his Father's house. He writes a hypocritical and spiteful answer to Father Jogues and spends the night with Agnes.

Their uneasy and tempestuous cohabitation lasts for some months — then Agnes breaks it off, as incomprehensibly in Richard's eyes as she had begun it. One morning he finds her lying mortally sick and in despair — but she shows him more tenderness than ever before. She gets well and goes away for a few days to the neighbouring village. And on her return it is as though she had never been his mistress. And when he claims his " right " to her, she strikes him across the face with her riding-whip.

In desperation he gets drunk at a tavern in the village, is involved in a brawl and arrested. There follows a grotesque travesty of justice. It dawns at last on Richard Fitzsimon how immeasurably he is hated as a Papist Cavalier and how delighted they are to have got their claws into him in the end. He is ready to die for the faith which he has not followed in his life. They laugh at him — nobody is going to do him any harm, they only want to teach him who he is, for his own good. He is publicly flogged and put in the pillory.

While he is still lying there half-conscious, an Indian comes and whispers to him that his friends are in the forest near by — some black gowns and a body of Christian Indians from Canada. They have come to seek an alliance with the local Mohicans against the Iroquois. And to rescue Fitzsimon.

Maltreated so that Agnes can hardly recognize him and half-crazy, he staggers home to the farm in the course of the night. Exultingly he tells his faithless mistress that there are others who have not failed him, the hour of vengeance has struck. She is beside herself with terror — the Indians! He has brought the Indians down upon the settlement! This leads to a scene in which they abuse each other unsparingly. And it ends in her consenting to accompany him — into the primeval forest, with the Jesuits, out into the unknown.

So he finds his way to the priests' camp hand in hand with his mistress and calls upon Father Jogues to marry them on the spot.

The priest refuses. Richard ought to know without being told that a man cannot be admitted to a great sacrament without confession, without piety, without grace. " Very well, then let me confess," Richard insists.

At a little distance from the campfire, behind a great stone, Richard kneels before the priest and confesses the whole story of his apostasy. " Hast thou heard this last, father? " he asks the silent priest, himself amazed now that he has to set out in words all that has happened. " I have heard, my son; go you on! " But at last there is an end of it. Father Jogues says he can only give him absolution on one condition: " If I bid you in God's name, send this woman away, and come with us, will ye

do it? " " Father," Richard replies wearily, " whatever
you command me that I will do, but would God I had
died today before 'twas asked of me." " 'Tis well. I will
absolve you and marry you too."

The little company starts on its journey through the
forests. The Canadians had never thought of making
any attack on the settlement. Richard realizes afterwards that Agnes has seen from the first the hopelessness
of their undertaking. She seems another woman, gentle,
patient, and submissive, since she knows the end to be
near, and so they can at least die together. It is soon
apparent that they will not be able to cross the Connecticut River — the Iroquois are on the war path on
the opposite bank. They have to turn back and take
refuge with their new allies, the Mohicans, for the present. Neither the Jesuits nor their Christian Abenakis
understand much of the Mohican language. But with
growing alarm they are all aware that something is brew-
ing.

Then the Mohicans make a sudden assault on the
settlement. Richard and some of the Abenakis try to
come to the relief of the colonists. He arrives just in
time to see a little of the horrors — and knows that for
all time they will be attributed to himself and the
Jesuits. He hurries back to Fleming's farm — it is in
flames. Among the ruins he finds Captain Gideon and
kills him in single combat. In the forest hard by he
finds Fleming dying under the Mohicans' tortures —
with his last breath the Scotsman curses " the Jesuit "

who has betrayed the colonists to the redskins and dies without hearing in what way Richard has betrayed him. And as Richard tries to hold Agnes back lest she should see how frightfully her father has been dealt with, she is shot down by the flying Mohicans.

As she dies she confesses that she has loved Richard more deeply than he will ever be able to understand. But that morning when he found her mortally sick she had taken poison. She had hoped to bring about her own death, but all she achieved was to kill their child within her. And then she married Gideon — because she was afraid, and because she did not know how else to end the relations between them, and because she had thoughts of her father. Best that things have turned out thus — even though Gideon is now dead — if their love had been never so great, their natures were too different for them to have gone through life together.

On their hopeless journey onward through the forests Richard one day asks the priest:

" How was it that although I loved this woman dearly and have now such proof that she loved me, there should have been at all times such a strife and attrition of our two spirits, that we were cheated out of all the joy we promised ourselves, and now I am left with little save tears and sighs as mementoes of her? . . . Yes, even at its extremest hours, when my arms were round the woman, her lips to mine, and all our kisses ran into one as the rain drops from a roof run into a stream, what was it, but as though I embraced a cage, wherein, untamed and untouched, her spirit fluttered and kept aloof from the violence of my desire? Why was it that I was never happy? Was it a lack of my nature to enjoy or of the thing itself to satisfy?"

"Marriage, Richard," says Father Jogues, "for I will call that marriage although therein ye sought not God's blessing until so late — marriage may be either of two things. . . . To a carnal heart, the ultimate of this world's delusions; to a spiritual, the poignantest realisation of eternity. The attraction of woman for man goeth far beyond the senses, even for the most brutal, though he know it not and would scoff at it if 'twere told him. Consciously or no, believe me, there is none but feeleth the transitoriness, the unsubstantiality of the world a burden upon his spirit, since, turn he where he will, all things remind him of his pilgrimage; that which he would possess for ever is but leased to him for a season; that which he would stay to serve his pleasure and ends, passeth on to serve and seek its own. This is the famous melancholia of love, Richard; this is the unappeasable desire of possession. That one living creature encountered by chance, first wistfully regarded, then loved, then coveted, standeth unto mankind a symbol for all the world. Can they but have and hold it, then the world escapes them no longer; lo! the intangible hath been touched, the incorporeal become flesh, the unattainable been attained. You have confessed to me yourself that when you saw this poor woman, you said to your heart, ' Here is peace for me at last within her arms; here is an end of all my toils and journeys.' But the end, Richard, is not here; the end is in heaven. The most blessed, the most favoured, the most congenial of wedded lives are naught but a sore and toilsome pilgrimage toward it, hand in hand. As for those others upon whom God's blessing rests not — what shall be said of them? They are swimmers from a wreck, that cling in one another's arms, and drown together, two by two."

A little group of readers, however, had discovered Stuart's book and appreciated it in such a way that they could never forget it. And the post-war period, the pressure of chaotic social conditions on men's minds, has by degrees opened the eyes of many to the horror and beauty of life and the mystery of the soul sufficiently to extend to wider circles a comprehension of the spiritual realism of a book like *Weeping Cross*. In 1933 a new edition was published and voices are not lacking to predict that it will live as an outstanding work in American fiction.

2

CROSBY HALL near Liverpool has been in the possession of the Blundell family since the twelfth century. For five generations the owners of Crosby rode from their home to be imprisoned on account of their faith — in Lancaster, Liverpool, Chester, or London. One and all

they were "most obstinate and stiff-necked recusants."
So far as I know, all the Blundells of Crosby have clung
to the faith of their fathers and paid the price of such
fidelity. It was the present Mr. Blundell of Crosby,
Member of Parliament, who in 1926 brought in the bill
the passing of which removed some of the last of Catholic Englishmen's civil disabilities.

Of the mass of letters, diaries and business papers preserved in the family archives a good deal has been
published by local historical societies and historians. In
addition to these there is Miss Margaret Blundell's edition of William Blundell's letters, furnished with a biographical commentary. This is a perfectly charming and
extremely enjoyable book.[1] In the first place of course
it is a gift to the Catholics of England; but it ought also
to find a place in any Catholic library in Scandinavia.

William Blundell was born in 1620 and died in 1698.
He lost his father when a child, so presumably it was
his grandfather who arranged the marriage between his
grandson and Sir Thomas Haggerston's daughter Anne.
Both children were in their fifteenth year when their
guardians tucked them into the nuptial bed together,
like putting dolls into a box. But the marriage of these
two docile, pious, and brave little people turned out in
a way that makes one think of the words of Our Lord
that "their angels in heaven always see the face of My

---

1 *Cavalier: Letters of William Blundell to His Friends, 1620–98*,
edited by Margaret Blundell (New York and London: Longmans, Green
& Company; 1933).

Father." They helped each other in imperturbable affection and loyal concord through a long and difficult life. So it is not surprising that William Blundell, in letters to his children and grandchildren, expresses his firm conviction that marriages arranged by parents and guardians are most likely to turn out happily.

No easy life was in store for William and Anne Blundell — that is very sure. Twenty years later he writes to his sister-in-law, Margaret Haggerston, in a letter which he himself calls " fantastical ":

" For you well remember what a pretty straight young thing, all dashing in scarlet I came into Haggerston when you saw me last. But now, if you chance to hear a thing come — thump — thump — up your stairs like a knocker, God bless us, at midnight, look out confidently: a gross full body of an ell or more in the waist, with an old peruke clapped on a bald pate . . . ' By my truly,' you will say, ' and that is a great pity.' And by my troth, sister, it is so; but we will talk more of this when you see it."

Life had not dealt leniently with the handsome fair-haired lad. No portrait is in existence of Anne Blundell, *née* Haggerston — all that is known of her appearance is that she was small and delicately built — but we may suppose she looked no less worn at this time; they were both midway in the thirties.

William's grandfather died in 1638. " I was father of a child and mine own master (God knows) before eighteen years of age," he writes.

" If the heir of papists be a Protestant he shall be discharged of all penalties, charges, and incumbrances happening upon him in respect or by reason of his ancestors' recusancy. . . . But if the heir of a papist shall be or become a papist, such heir shall not be freed of the penalty," it is laid down in a statute of James I.

Two thirds of the Crosby estate were at this time sequestered by the Crown as covering for the fines — twenty pounds a month (the purchasing power of the pound was then about eight times what it is now) — owed by his ancestors for refusing to take part in Protestant church services. It was a punishable offence for parents to give their children a Catholic education; Catholic priests were outlawed, forced to baptize, instruct, wed, and bury the faithful in secret. Outside the Catholic's home the world was waiting, ready to bid him welcome and offer him a share in its joys and its honour, if he would " go over " to it. If he held fast to the faith of his fathers, he was, as William Blundell writes of his son, doomed to the plough and to trouble.

William's grandfather, however, had come to an agreement with the Crown, by which he was allowed to cultivate the neglected two thirds of his ancestral estate on payment of an annual rent to the King of thirty pounds. To begin with, the very young master took the rosiest view of life. Within the bounds of propriety he enjoyed himself to the full — from morning to night he was on the go, with field sports, hunting, riding his own racehorses, and, unfortunately, betting as though he had unlimited wealth at his command; he delighted to take part in all the fairs and rustic merrymakings which have marked the countryman's seasons since pagan antiquity, and which the Catholic Church has been careful to preserve and consecrate by means of holy festivals and popular devotions to the Giver of all good gifts. Before William Blundell had grown much older, Cromwell's government was to reach out its hard hand to suppress and if possible uproot all such manifestations of man's primeval joy in feeling that, after all, life may be a lovely thing, in spite of sin and sorrow and dangers — and even if we have turned God's green earth into a vale of tears, there are moments when all normal people discover how well all things were created in the beginning, and how, thank God, we have not succeeded in ruining the earth entirely.

Perhaps it is precisely this that is the secret of William Blundell's nature, as shown in his letters: he always takes this view of the world. A vale of tears; it cannot be otherwise, once sin has entered into it. And its prince in this age is a usurper who can create nothing himself and therefore strives to destroy the masterpiece of Another. But the world *is* God's work; the Evil One may do his worst, he will never succeed in destroying its goodness and beauty altogether. And moreover the home of the believers is in heaven; here on earth they are merely passing through. In his heart of hearts his religion is the only thing that William Blundell takes with unshakable seriousness. However difficult and des-

perate his worldly affairs may be, his humour, his lively
interest in everything and everyone around him, his
pungent wit, are always awake — everything that comes
his way is an adventure on the road. When the journey
is ended all these things will be worth remembering.

He soon discovered that his sporting tastes had cost
him more than a Catholic landowner could afford, when
he had to support a wife, a growing flock of children,
and two unmarried sisters, besides paying regular fines
for " recusancy." As long as he lived he had to smart
for the two short years in which he had thoroughly enjoyed himself, before he was really grown up. Before
long his difficulties were to be increased. William Blundell records them in all brevity:

" The war between King Charles and his Parliament
began A.D. 1642. That year (1642–3) 18th March my
thigh was broken in the King's service. Anno Domini
1643 all my lands and most of my goods were sequestered
for being a Papist and Delinquent (as the prevailing
part called the King's partakers). In the year 1645 my
wife farmed my demesne of Crosby. And all her quick
goods being lost, she bought one horse and two oxen, to
make up a team."

All warlike and peaceful professions in England had
long been closed to Catholics — in every case an oath
was required denying the Pope's supremacy in spiritual
matters. But in the autumn of 1642 Charles I granted
Catholics the right to take up arms in defence of his

cause. At the same time he gave a solemn promise to the Parliament never to pardon a Catholic priest under sentence of death without the consent of both Houses. And in fact the year 1642 saw eight priests executed for high treason when the indictment against them concerned nothing more than administering the sacraments of the Church contrary to law. Nevertheless the Catholics flocked to the King's standards. William Blundell received his captain's commission, which empowered him to raise a troop of a hundred dragoons at his own expense. This made an end of the family silver from Crosby Hall. Blundell distinguished himself at the storming of Lancaster, March 17, but as he fought his way into the town his thigh was broken by a cannon-ball. While the wounded Cavalier was moved from house to house among his friends, Crosby Hall was looted so thoroughly, he records, " that the bread which my children ate was buried in the ground, thereby to preserve it for them from one meal to another."

For a whole year after the storming of Lancaster Blundell was helpless, suffering from his wound. At last the leg was mended, more or less, but it was now sadly shorter than the other, and he was known as " Halt Will " for the rest of his life.

After the Royalist defeat at Naseby the Parliament confiscated all the estates of the landed gentry who had fought in Charles's armies. William Blundell was compelled to hide among the mountains of Wales, sometimes disguised as a woman — a number of his letters of this period are signed " Cicely Burton." It was now that he got into the way of using his enforced leisure to supplement the studies he was unable to complete in his youth. As a result of the many imprisonments he suffered in the course of his long life he had the reputation at his death of being an exceedingly learned old gentleman.

Meanwhile his young wife was living at Crosby with five little children — one they had already lost — and two sisters-in-law, not yet grown up. Mrs. Blundell claimed her right according to law to occupy the dwelling-house at Crosby; she farmed the confiscated lands and at the same time applied for the return of a fifth part of the estate, which the wife of a recusant was entitled to claim for the support of herself and her children. William appears to have paid an occasional furtive visit to his home. And in 1647 he was a prisoner on parole in his own house — with the right to wear a sword for the protection of his family, on account of the insecurity of the times. It appears too that the lame gentleman was obliged to avail himself of this right. And the Roundheads' prisoner kept Christmas together with his family and a few friends in a manner that was utterly ungodly and abominable in the eyes of the victorious party; among other things they acted a play, and at the request of his neighbours William Blundell composed a little rhymed prologue to the entertainment.

The children must have been too young to take part in the play on that occasion. But for the Christmas of 1663 their father wrote a piece for his little girls " for to embolden them in speaking." It is tremendously serious and moralizing to begin with: her father exhorts his little Mall to discipline and earnestness and good behaviour, to prayer and meditation. And this makes so strong an impression on Mall that when her younger sisters appear on the stage she immediately passes on the instruction she has received. But Frances and Bridget and Betty show no signs of reform — they roar with laughter at their converted sister, and that brings the comedy to an end!

But with New Year 1648, when the Royalists essayed a final campaign, fresh difficulties set in for Squire Blundell. He had to fly from home several times, finally to the Isle of Man — the last refuge of the Cavaliers. Here Blundell began to write the history of Man — a work which was first printed in 1876 by the Manx Society. But then he felt he could not leave his brave wife to shift for herself in those bad times. In the following summer Blundell was absorbed in a nursery garden he had laid out. He sowed cherry stones in a bed " finely wrought for that purpose. There came up no cherry trees, but in place thereof a pretty crop of ash plants." From this the amateur gardener concluded that the cherry stones must have come from trees which had been grafted on ash stems, " for the seed of fruit will produce a tree agreeable to the stock or root from whence it came," he remarks.

The years following King Charles's capture and death were full of trouble for Blundell. And the misery prevailing in the country round him cut the impoverished Cavalier to the heart. His old farmers and the humble folk of Lancashire were in great part faithful Catholics. As time went on they were unable to pay the fines for absenting themselves from the services of the State Church; they had to leave house and home and were reduced to beggary. (Many of the English martyr priests came from humble Catholic homes of this sort.) — And at Crosby the flock of children was growing. William and Anne Blundell had fourteen children in all. Four of them died in infancy. The father took their deaths calmly — it seems almost as if he thought these innocent little souls had in their own way spoken with God about the matter: they were better fitted to pass straight into heaven and from thence to help their relatives with their prayers. The ten he was permitted to keep would thus be better equipped for the trying life, full of struggles and losses and efforts, which awaited the Catholic boys and girls of England in those troubled times.

Their parents entirely disregarded the prohibitions against giving children a Catholic education, and against harbouring Catholic priests. In 1652 a Jesuit, Father John Walton, was living at Crosby. He was probably tutor to Squire Blundell's boys while at the same time he cared in secret for the souls of the Catholics in the neighbourhood. A price was set on the head of every Catholic priest, and Catholic country houses were constantly troubled, day and night, by the visits of priest-hunters, but Father Walton contrived to live in peace at Crosby.

The house of course had its secret hiding-place, the " priest hole," in the wall between two rooms, and the impracticable hills of Wales were not so very far away.

Meanwhile it was absolutely necessary that Blundell should take some steps to secure his family's daily bread and to try to save Crosby Hall for his kin. He was helped by a cousin who was a Protestant and by a Protestant lawyer. The Parliament was in need of money and offered for sale the confiscated estates of Catholic landowners. It tried indeed to prevent Protestants acting as a cloak for their Catholic neighbours and relatives. Nevertheless in a great many cases family ties and neighbourly good feeling proved stronger than the Parliament's vigilance. William Blundell was able to raise loans and actually to buy back the greater part of the Crosby lands, though his friends remained the nominal owners until the restoration of the monarchy seven years later. But Halt Will was terribly cramped by debts and interest during these years, and bitterly repented the extravagances of his merry young days.

Accounts and notebooks tell us that William Blundell was an energetic agriculturist. He brought limestone from Wales for top-dressing his land — sowed barley one year, then let the land lie fallow for a year, sowed wheat the next and had full crops, he writes.

The voluminous Recipe Book from Crosby is no doubt mainly the work of the women. There are receipts for food and drink, for pastry and soap, for medicines and ointments to cure pretty nearly all the ills that flesh is heir to here on earth, and for simple cosmetics whereby those of the girls who survived the home-made medicines might improve their appearance. The remedies consisted of all English wild or cultivated flowers and herbs kept in spirit, of the ashes of " young ravons " and powdered human skulls (it is noted that young ravens may be difficult to obtain, but no such remark is made about the skulls!) ; boiled snails and pounded hares' feet, yellow wax and tobacco ash, yolk of egg and steel filings figure in the most remarkable combinations. For internal use the ingredients are usually taken in sack or rosewater. That ten out of fourteen children survived these cures is hard to understand.

At this time we begin to hear of William Blundell's sister Mistress Frances. She soon becomes one of the leading figures in the family history. — There is of course some truth in the many harrowing tales we hear of the unhappy lot of unmarried sisters in old days, just as there are good grounds for the legend of the old maiden aunts' reign of terror before our time. Whether the old maids were trampled on or themselves did the trampling depended partly on the character of the ladies and partly on what sort of relatives they had to deal with. Frances Blundell must have been born masterful. But she exerted her power exclusively for the good of the family. " The strongest spoke in the wheel of our fortune," her brother calls her in their old days.

She is thirty-three when William for the first time sketches her character in a letter to his mother-in-law —

whom Frances is visiting and who is unwilling to let her go, though the people at Crosby are so badly off without Sister Frances. To her delicate sister Winifred she gave a husband's protection, to Anne she was companion and assistant, she was little Milly's teacher and her brother's indispensable partner in the interesting game of shuttle-cock. She comes off with flying colours, whether Lady Haggerston sets her to storm a goose pasty as thick as the castle wall or to play games with the other young ladies. But William must invoke his mother-in-law's forbearance — she will have to release Frances soon, for they cannot do without her at Crosby Hall.

Frances therefore was charged with the instruction of the little girls at Crosby. The birch-rod played an important part in seventeenth-century education, and it looks as if the little Blundells, boys and girls alike, received ample doses of the rod for sins and misdemeanours great and small. In the little Christmas play " Father," to prove how fond he is of his children, reminds them that he has given " Mall " thrashings without end. In the piece, however, Mall undauntedly answers that her father must surely know how often in confession both she and he have admitted the same sins, have promised to reform and prayed to God for strength to put off their evil ways. And God has given them remission of their sins, but all the same they have both " done it again." Whereupon " Father " lets the sharp-witted youngster off this time. — Life was stern; both grown-ups and children were used to harsh treatment — the old family papers from Crosby bear witness that affection between parents and children was nevertheless deep and tender and heartfelt, and their mutual understanding in the matters which affected their lives most profoundly was as great as is humanly possible.

William Blundell's eldest son, Nicholas, heir to Crosby, was smuggled over to France at the age of fifteen, to enter the college of English Jesuits at Saint-Omer. Shortly afterwards his father had to go to prison in Liverpool, as he had not been able to pay all the fines and taxes, ordinary and extraordinary, to which Crosby was liable. From the prison he managed to send a letter to his aunt, Elizabeth Bradshaigh, who was a nun in the convent of the Poor Clares at Rouen. His eldest daughter, Jane, longed " to be serviceable to that good Family into which you have devoted yourself." The meaning of this was that Jane desired to take the veil. As soon as Blundell was released from prison he applied for permission to go to London (according to law, Catholics required special permission to travel more than five miles from their place of residence — in his letters Blundell alludes to this distance of five miles as " his chain ").

Permission was granted. Jane's younger sister, the fifteen-year-old Margaret, wished to accompany her to the convent. And it appears that their father, presumably disguised and under an assumed name, was fortunate enough to be able to conduct his daughters across the Channel and as far as the convent gate. He writes in his notebook:

" My daughter Margaret, in the fifteenth year of her age, seeing some exquisite cuts of white marble upon the graves of some great persons in that ancient church of Tongre, asked me if they were not all saints? I told her I hoped that many of them were good men and therefore might probably be now saints. ' Why,' said she, ' are not all these which we see incorrupted bodies? ' "

So thoroughly was the prohibition of religious sculpture enforced in England that obviously little Margaret had never seen a statue of a saint before.

The letters from the father of thirty-eight to his daughter of eighteen in the convent show that, although the relations between parents and children at that time were formal enough and in general the children were kept at a respectful distance, in the sphere of religion they met in profound and intimate mutual understanding — and here the father, while speaking frankly to his child about his own religious life, refrains from giving her too much advice; in the place where she now is she will soon have more experience of such things than he has himself.

In 1660 Nicholas informed his father that he wished to renounce his right of inheritance and enter the Society of Jesus. By this act Nicholas Blundell rendered himself an outlaw in his native land, liable to the death penalty and with a price on his head if he came to England. But his father willingly released Nicholas and allowed him to follow his exalted and perilous calling.

" ' We'll hang them,' sayeth a Lancaster jury. ' We'll crown them,' sayeth Christ," wrote William Blundell of the Jesuits.

He came home after having accompanied the two girls to the Clares and had to betake himself at once to " his old lodging in the town of Liverpool " — the prison. Mistress Anne sent woodcock pies and butter to the families in London who had looked after her girls on their journey.

This time Blundell had a new companion in his imprisonment: Richard Butler, eldest son of Viscount Mountgarret, who had been a zealous supporter of the Royalist cause in Ireland. No doubt young Butler had come to England on a secret mission — now that Oliver Cromwell was dead the Royalists were actively scheming for the restoration of the monarchy. This time both Blundell and Butler were released fairly soon, and the young Irish gentleman accompanied the other to Crosby. He and the seventeen-year-old Emelia Blundell instantly fell in love with each other.

It required less knowledge of human nature than William Blundell possessed to see that Lord Mountgarret would never hear of a match between his eldest son and the daughter of a ruined country gentleman who was without title or rank, even if he belonged to one of the oldest families in England. He sent Emelia to an aunt and wrote to Mountgarret's lawyer in London, asking for money for Richard Butler — for the young man hadn't a farthing and could not leave Crosby till he had paid his debts in Liverpool and provided himself with clothes and a horse. What Blundell was not prepared for was that Mountgarret's wrath should fall upon the host who had taken charge of his son when the latter was destitute. The Irish nobleman's insulting letters stirred the patient, good-natured Englishman for once to red-hot fury. And the mere fact that Richard Butler had dared to think of marrying on his own responsibility was enough for Mountgarret to cast him off. He was given just as much money as would pay his debts in the town, but he had to leave Crosby on his two feet, with a small sum that Blundell had provided for his journey.

After Butler had tried for three years to make shift without support from his angry father, he turned up again at Crosby and renewed his wooing of Emelia Blundell; " whether love alone or rather his great distress have persuaded him to this I am not able to say," writes William Blundell. This time, however, it ended in his giving his consent, and Emelia Blundell became Mistress Emelia Butler. In reality Lord Mountgarret's financial difficulties were just as desperate as those of most other Royalists, so he had several good reasons for remaining irreconcilable. Blundell had to house the young Butlers for five years, and even to find the money for his son-in-law's clothes and his manservant's wages. The number of mouths that Squire Blundell had to feed from the produce of his farm was increased by four little Butlers during these years. He kept at it, clearing more land

and liming his worst fields with good results. At any rate, since the accession of Charles II he was again in possession of his own estate, in name as well as in fact.

The ruined Catholic Cavaliers had been entirely excluded from the moves which led to the restoration of the monarchy. But the weakness of the government during Richard Cromwell's Protectorate and after his abdication had, in practice if not in theory, made life a little easier for the proscribed. In 1660 Blundell had been able to accompany his youngest son Thomas to Saint-Omer and to return through Holland, where, lame though he was, he had amused himself by ascending various church towers and had an opportunity in Breda of seeing the children of his murdered King playing bowls one Sunday morning.

It proved that the new King dared not do anything to reward the Catholic adherents of the Stuart cause or to lighten the lot of " Popish recusants." On the contrary, the Conventicle Act of 1664 made it penal for more than five persons outside a family to take part in religious services which were not prescribed in the Church of England prayer-book. Ever since Elizabeth's days, when it was made high treason to take part in the holy Mass, this had been secretly celebrated in the chapel at Crosby, which had served as parish church for all the Catholics of the neighbourhood. So now William Blundell was threatened with further fines and obliged to practise his religion with even greater caution than before. His letters about his most intimate interests and about the weal and woe of his nearest and dearest friends are now even fuller of circumlocution and obscure figures of speech. Apparently these letters were sometimes sent wrapped in the famous game pies from the Crosby kitchen.

In the course of his attempts to get his son-in-law's Irish relations to do something to help the young family, he found at last a friend in Lord Mountgarret's London lawyer, Mr. Langhorne. Langhorne's infinitely tactful and efficient kindness was one of the brightest spots in the Blundell family's existence, until in 1679 the Blessed Richard Langhorne won the martyr's crown as one of the victims of Titus Oates's plot.

In 1665, while the plague was raging in London, Blundell's fourth and sixth daughters, Alice and Mary, went to the convent of English Augustinian nuns at Bruges, Alice on probation for entering the Order, Mary — the badly behaved Mall — in order to receive a little more education. Later on they both joined the Poor Clares at Gravelines. As life was beginning to shape itself in England under the rule of the Merry Monarch, serious Catholic Christians could only view it with anxiety and repugnance. After the bigotry and puritanical hostility to life of the preceding regime men's repressed instincts found vent in a coarse and unrestrained pursuit of pleasure. Blundell writes in 1665 to his sister-in-law:

" Madam, I am a wretched poor creature: Age and Infirmity, Debts and cares are growing daily upon me, and that which is the worst of all, my own great vanities and my pride have occasioned the most of my troubles. If I be not able to mend my fortunes I trust I shall mend my life, and I do not despair (by the assistance of your good prayers) either of the one or the other. I am likewise a grand Malcontent (as Others in want are) and I love retirement. As often as I am forced from my nest I return thither again with amazement and Horror, having discovered too much of the riotous unhappy courses even of those kind of men, among the rest, unto whom the safety of this Nation is in a great measure entrusted. And Madam I do heartily give thanks to God that my own weak condition hath disabled me to be a Sinner at so costly a rate. . . . And now when I speak of your Ark (at Haggerston) I must here acknowledge that the Dove which was sent from thence some 30 years ago hath saved from sinking our little cockboat at Crosby in many a storm. . . . It is my hard fortune now to become an useless servant to your family, as being wholly a slave to my own."

William Blundell never forgot that after God he had to thank his wife above all for their being still in possession of Crosby Hall. It is no disparagement of the heroic lady's achievement to say that her case was by no means unique in her age — or in any age. And yet there are women calling themselves feminists who venture to assert that women have made no contribution to history before they themselves began to do their best to achieve barrenness!

Nevertheless in 1666 the state of things at Crosby had become so embarrassing that William Blundell had to

try to come to some arrangement about his " son Butler's " affairs. He went over to Ireland — and wrote harrowing descriptions of the poverty and scarcity in that
country — got in touch with his son-in-law's relatives,
and found them not unwilling to take charge of the
young couple. Only Lord and Lady Mountgarret were
irreconcilable. But in spite of this the Butlers crossed
over in 1667. The husband was ill, the wife was expect-
ing her fifth child, nothing definite awaited them. Aunt
Frances accompanied them and joined battle with the
stony-hearted grandmother, Lady Mountgarret, who was
not to be softened even when Mistress Frances brought
two of the grandchildren for her to see. At last through
the intervention of the Duke of Ormond the Butlers
were given a house to live in on the family property in
Kilkenny. But they remained miserably poor. Even
when Richard Butler inherited the estates in 1679 and
became the fifth Viscount Mountgarret, his and Lady
Emelia's affairs were a constant source of sorrow and
anxiety to the old people at Crosby.

It was now time to find a wife for William Blundell
junior, Halt Will's second son, who was to carry on
the family, since both his elder and his younger brother
had entered the Society of Jesus. It was, by the way, a
Jesuit priest, Father Heaton, who finally arranged a suitable match with a Catholic young lady, Mary Eyre of
Hassop — the priests of that time had to assist their pa-
rishioners in a variety of ways. There could be no question of the newly married couple having a home of their

own, and soon three generations were living together at Crosby as one family. It was not long before her parents-in-law grew just as fond of Mistress Mary as of their own children. William Blundell the elder has nothing but good to say of her — that she is just as " teeming " as his own wife is evidently an added virtue in his eyes. His only worry is that she is not particularly strong. During her repeated pregnancies she suffered from " convulsive fitts " — and presumably had to undergo all the fearsome cures for that ailment which are set out in the family receipt-book. In spite of it all she survived her thirteen confinements, closed her husband's eyes, and had sufficient vitality to feel a call to the cloistered life after she had been left a widow. One of her daughters was Abbess at Ghent, and under her the old lady ended her days as a nun.

After the son-in-law was settled in Ireland and the son married, there followed a couple of comparatively peaceful years at Crosby. Blundell's chief trouble was that of assuring his daughter Frances the minimum " dowry " which a postulant had to contribute to the poor English convents on the Continent. Her father writes to his old friend Father Walton, who has sent him news, among other things of marriages within the circle of their friends:

" There is a girl of mine for whom I am treating of another manner of match; the contract should be on the other side o' the sea; her Spouse will neither die nor displease her."

By the Treaty of Dover in 1670 King Charles, in return for large subsidies from King Louis XIV, had secretly pledged himself to become a Catholic and to support France with troops in the war with Holland. As a *ballon d'essai* the King issued in 1672 a declaration which was to secure liberty of conscience to Catholics. This raised a storm of fury, and in its place Parliament passed the Test Act, by which no one could hold an office under the Crown unless he took an oath which condemned among other things the belief in transubstantiation. From the King's brother, the Lord High Admiral, afterwards King James II, and the Lord High Treasurer, Baron Clifford, downwards, every single Catholic was expelled from his position in the military and civil services, and Parliament demanded that the penal laws against Catholics should be enforced with full severity — they had long remained a dead letter in many cases, such as those of persons who in general had shown themselves to be good and loyal Englishmen.

" We are all here for the present in a most dreadful high suspense," Blundell writes to the Abbess of the Poor Clares at Rouen; " concerning the late rigorous proclamation and threats against our lives and fortunes. We have not known the like with so many great circumstances of terror, in 20 years last past. God grant us patience and perseverance and His will be done on earth as it is in Heaven."

Aunt Frances, who was already used to crossing between England and Ireland on all sorts of unpleasant errands and in all weathers, accompanied Frances to Rouen. Five of William Blundell's daughters had now chosen to go into exile and serve God in the cloister. At Crosby a new generation swarmed into the world. The grandfather had retained the Butlers' eldest little boy when his parents left, and had taken charge of his education. Edmund Butler was evidently the favourite of all at Crosby; Aunt Frances was like a mother to him. But the state of affairs in England now looked so threatening that the old maid took her treasure over to Kilkenny. Before long, however, the Butlers sent both him and his younger brother Richard back to Crosby — they could not afford to keep them. Blundell managed to scrape together enough money to send the elder to the college at Saint-Omer. Shortly after, Father Nicholas Blundell, S.J., returned to his native land, which was now to be the field of his labours, in disguise, under an assumed name, and outlawed. The law that Catholics might not absent themselves more than a few miles from their domicile had lately been enforced so strictly that for the present his father and mother could have no hope of seeing their eldest son. Not till the summer of 1678 was Father Blundell able to visit the old home which he had left twenty-three years before. For four or five weeks he remained concealed at Crosby, and in the little domestic chapel his nearest relatives and his old neighbours and friends with their families received the sacraments from the hands of Nicholas Blundell. He returned to London in order to be present at the festival of July 25 — St. James's day — when the fathers of the English province each year renew their vows. The Provincial, Father Whitebread, preached on the day's text, St. Matthew xx, 22:

" Can you undergo a hard persecution, be falsely betrayed and injured, and hurried away to prison? *Possumus.* We can, blessed be God. *Potestis bibere calicem quem ego bibiturus sum?* Can you suffer the hardships of a gaol? Can you sleep on straw and live on hard diet? Can you lie in chains and fetters? Can you endure the rack? *Possumus.* We can, blessed be God. *Potestis bibere calicem quem ego bibiturus sum?* Can you be brought to the bar and hear yourself falsely sworn against? Can you patiently receive the sentence of an unjust judge, condemning you to a painful death, to be hung, drawn, and quartered? *Possumus.* We can."

Just then Titus Oates was busily engaged in fabricating his indictment of the Jesuits, accusing them of a plot to murder the King and overthrow the government — Titus Oates, whom Macaulay calls " the falsest, the most malignant, and the most impudent being that ever disgraced the human form, the founder of a school of false witnesses." With the psychiatric knowledge of our day it is easy enough to determine that Titus Oates was an entirely abnormal, perverse, and pitiable human wreck — and as regards " human form " his portraits exhibit a horribly mis-shapen type which may be found in certain medical works. It was on the fantastic accusations of this miserable wretch that so many courageous and holy men had to lose their lives on the gallows, so many families were ruined, so many victims were subjected to torture and thrown into prisons where they often lay forgotten and were allowed to languish year after year, if they did not die of jail fever or some other of the diseases that were rife in the dungeons of that age.

Even then there were many intelligent people in England who had no doubt that Oates and his collaborators were lying and that the whole business was the invention of half-insane fanatics of more than doubtful morality. (Oates had been expelled from his offices in the Church of England and also from Catholic colleges as an incurable pæderast.) King Charles saw clearly how the matter stood. But he dared not do otherwise than sign death warrant after death warrant — hatred of the Jesuits and fear of the " Papist danger " had assumed the character of a mass psychosis and the opponents of the house of Stuart exploited the popular excitement to the utmost.

Father Nicholas Blundell was one of the Jesuits whom Oates accused and, as it happened, was the fortuitous means of unmasking his untrustworthiness to some extent: it appeared that Oates had pointed out a Benedictine, Father Caryll, one of the Queen's chaplains, to his hue and cry in mistake for the Jesuit Blundell, whereupon the proceedings against Caryll were abandoned. Father Blundell escaped. But among the victims was the lawyer Richard Langhorne. His meditations in prison on death and eternity have lately been published by the Catholic Truth Society as a book of devotion.

Once more William Blundell had to make over the greater part of his property to Protestant friends, who then paid the nominal interest of the purchase money to Mrs. Anne Blundell. Again she had to act as the " dove " that saved the ark of Crosby, while her husband was once more a fugitive. For a long time he applied in vain for a passport to enable him to leave the country, taking with him his grandson, Richard Butler. At first it looked as if he would be unable to obtain it save on the unacceptable condition that he was not to return to England without express permission. It was natural that the old man, who had been maimed in the service of the King's father and had fought all his life to preserve his family seat in spite of fines and threats and worries, should now at last feel bitter. But he toiled at home as steadfastly as ever, observing the passage of the seasons around him with the same affectionate attention as in other years:

" 30th January 1680. White violets were plucked in my garden, and Daffodils in great number budded and near breaking out; as to the flower, plenty of tansy about a finger long. And on the first of February many of our Aprecock buds were red. Some hawthorn leaves were in February as broad as a silver twopence, many were so. On the 30th of March 1680 very many of my summer russeting apple blossom were full blown. Our pear trees fully flowered and in their greatest lustre, March 25th 1680."

In April 1680 Squire Blundell and his grandson at last were able to leave for the Continent.

Father Nicholas Blundell had just died at Saint-Omer, at the age of forty — no doubt as a result of his imprisonment in the previous year. But William Blundell was able to speak to his five daughters through the grating of the Clares' convent and to bid them good-bye till they met again in heaven. He continued his journey to Paris, but had to leave again in order to take care of Edmund Butler, who had been attacked by smallpox in the college. The grandfather's anxiety for the lad was tinged with worries — where was he to find the money to meet these expenses? The only sure thing was that the father, Lord Mountgarret, would make no contribution. In any case the lad recovered, and in the following year Blundell returned to Crosby. His letters show not only that he had heartily enjoyed his stay in a country where he was free to practise his religion, but that he also looked back with pleasure to the wine and the lighter air, now that he had returned to the home-brewed ale and the fogs of Crosby.

That winter he was so ill that a doctor from Wigan was summoned, who reinforced the arsenal of medicaments with drugs to the value of £5, 5s., 3d. Blundell took a lively interest in studying the effect of all these substances on his old frame. He recovered from his illness. But in 1685 Anne Blundell died.

No letters or other documents exist in which the widower speaks of his loss or of his life during the period following his wife's death. It looks as if for a long time he was not equal to pursuing his usual mode of life.

Charles II died — as a Catholic; an hour or two before his death he made his confession of faith and was able to receive the sacraments of the Church before expiring. James II ascended the throne, and immediately the penal laws against Catholics became inoperative, though they did not disappear from the statute-book. In spite of his previously expressed reluctance to be absent from Crosby, William Blundell now began to make frequent journeys to London and long stays in that city. Among other things he pursued historical studies there and wrote constantly to his son Thomas Blundell, S.J., about the history of the family and of Crosby Hall. He also permitted himself another little trip abroad, to Flanders and France. He came home immediately before the new storm burst upon the Catholics of England, with the expulsion of King James and the usurpation of the throne by the Prince of Orange.

Again the prisons were filled with recusants — although the new King had proclaimed that their lives and property would be spared — and the air of London and the surrounding districts was thick with the smoke of Catholics' houses consigned to the flames. Again William Blundell was thrown into prison — he was now a man of seventy — and the legal provision that no Catholic might own a horse whose value exceeded five pounds led to the stables of Crosby being plundered. Scarcely was he released from one prison when he was taken to

another. This last incarceration was no doubt due to
the fact that his grandson Edmund Butler had been
taken prisoner when leading an attack on Londonderry
and to his having written a letter from prison to his
grandfather concerning his warlike exploits, specially
charging him to tell Aunt Frances all about them and to
give her his affectionate greetings. In Manchester jail
Blundell passed the time by translating a French book
of devotion into English. No sooner was he set free
again than he and Mistress Frances exerted themselves
to the utmost to assist Captain Butler.

The son-in-law Mountgarret seems to have had about
as much affection for his sons as his own father had had
for him. The last years of William Blundell's life were
largely occupied in caring for the young Butlers — sup-
plying them with money, endeavouring to reconcile
them with their father, advising them in their matri-
monial plans. Richard, the younger, had been a scatter-
brained lad and continued to give anxiety to his grandfather by his incurable frivolity. He married a widow,
Lady Hamilton, who was decidedly his senior, and old
Blundell hoped he would allow himself to be guided
by the lady. The old man carefully put away the happy
bridegroom's accounts of her excellent qualities, thinking that if Mr. Richard should change his mind his own
letters would be there to witness against him.

It was now William Blundell junior who got up before
the sun and slaved from dawn to eve in order to support
them all at Crosby. In 1694 he and seven other gentle-

men from Lancashire were arrested and arraigned for high treason. A disciple of Oates, a former highwayman named Lunt, alleged he had discovered a conspiracy the object of which was to murder King William and bring back King James with the aid of French troops — a point which should be well calculated to create another mass psychosis. Lunt and his fellow-conspirators, however, were a little too stupid. Besides other things, they had put into writing and signed an agreement as to the way in which the Catholic gentlemen's estates were to be divided among them. A youthful brother of one of the accused landowners won Lunt's confidence under an assumed name so effectually that he was let into the secret of the whole transaction and even promised a share in the expected booty. He then appeared under his own name as a witness for the defence and produced forged letters which Lunt, not very convincingly, had composed in King James's name. Lunt's past and that of his accomplices was closely examined. And when the accused were at last acquitted and released, the population of Manchester cheered them and drove their accusers out of the town with stones and hooting. William Blundell junior was able to ride home a free man, between his old father and his young daughter, who had both been examined in the course of the trial.

In the last years of his life William Blundell could no longer write; his hands were crippled by rheumatism. But the indefatigable sister Frances, writing to Lord Mountgarret's second wife — Lady Emelia was now dead — to get her to do something for her stepson James Butler, reveals that it was still their grandfather and herself on whom the young Butlers had to rely whenever they were in difficulties. James had been left to get on as best he could since he was a half-grown youth; he had served as a soldier in Flanders and been taken prisoner by Ormond, who had offered to engage the lad in his own troop. James could not accept the offer as he was a Catholic, but Ormond had then given him arms, clothes, money, and a passport, enabling him to return home to Crosby. As the young soldier was " more ignorant in knowledge of books or skill in his pen than can scarcely be imagined," they were willing to keep him and look after his education. But Mistress Frances asks his stepmother kindly if she cannot arrange for James to have a little money from home to complete his scanty wardrobe. Whether James Butler received any, history does not relate.

In 1697 William Blundell dictated to a servant his account of a terrible hailstorm which ravaged the neighbourhood on the evening of April 29 and broke most of the window-panes at Crosby — even the leads of the windows were bent and torn in many places. He concludes as follows:

" The heat that evening was so excessive great that a little before five of the clock, when I stood upon our little mount to look over the garden wall thinking I should behold an infinity of those hailstones lying on the fallowed grounds in the field directly under the wall, yet there was not so much as one stone to be seen but all were dissolved but such as lay in the shades."

That is the last we hear of William Blundell — that the old Cavalier stands in his garden looking out upon his fields, over which the storm has passed. But now the warmth of the sun has melted the hailstones everywhere — only a few were left in the shade.

In the following year he died, on May 24, 1698. No account has been left of his last illness and death. But several years earlier he had written in his notebook:

" While I am in health, I may do well to make and write down a prayer, protestation, or soliloquy, just such a one as I would desire to say in the extremity of my last sickness. By this I may renounce all thoughts, words and deeds contrary to a good Christian, which shall happen or to which I shall be tempted at the time. I may beg of God to assist my soul while my body lies in torment, and by the extreme anguish thereof hath stupefied or perverted my reason. I may beg likewise grace for my friends that stand by to assist me, that they may not be scandalised either at the rage or stupidity which may happen unto me by the force of the sickness. And I may offer myself up to suffer more and longer torments if it be God's pleasure I should do so; and that grace may be allowed me to bear them, I may carry this paper about me, to the end it may be read to me in my sickness."

(1935)

THE STRONGEST POWER

 AT nine o'clock on the morning of November 22, 1641 the House of Commons began to debate the protest addressed to King Charles I which is known in history by the name of the Grand Remonstrance. It contained an enumeration of all the accusations brought by the Opposition against the King — two hundred and forty points — and a single constructive idea: namely, that thereafter the King must choose as his Ministers only such men as the Commons approved of. That meant that the King was to hand over his ancient prerogative to an oligarchy, the new class of rich men whose interests the Commons represented, and deliver up the episcopal Church of England to Puritans of all shades. On one single thing they were all agreed — more or less, at any rate: in hating the very idea of doctrinal authority in the Church. Officially the resolution was proposed by a somewhat insignificant member of the House. But no one was in doubt that its

real fathers were Sir Henry Vane junior and Mr. Oliver Cromwell.

The debate lasted all day. Darkness came on, but there was a call for lights. The proceedings were resumed, and went on into the small hours. Then the protest was adopted by a majority of only eleven votes. It would not have passed if several of the Royalist members had not left one after another, as they were not equal to sitting any longer. The men of the Opposition were equal to it.

At about three o'clock Mr. Cromwell and Lord Falkland stepped out together into the dark and raw November night. Falkland had belonged to the Opposition party when it directed its attacks on the policy of the King and Strafford. But when the fanaticism of the sectarians was turned against the Church he went over to the King's side. Cromwell was greatly excited after the debate in the Commons. If the protest had been thrown out, he said, he would have sold all he possessed and left England for ever. Falkland replied that it had fallen out as it usually did: " They who hated the bishops hated them worse than the devil, and they who loved them did not love them so well as their dinner."

On the following New Year's Day Lord Falkland accepted the office of First Secretary of State; he bowed to the King's wish, but he can scarcely have regarded the future with much hope. All were ready for the civil war, no one desired it, and yet it came — the antagonisms between the ideals represented by the two parties, and the self-interests with which, consciously or unconsciously, human ideals are always entangled, were too great.

It was not inclination but a sense of duty that had drawn Lucius Cary, Lord Falkland, into politics. His inclination was for the life from which he had torn himself away when he thought his country required it. At his seat, Great Tew, Falkland, who was himself a philosopher and writer, had gathered a circle of scholars, jurists, theologians, naturalists, and philosophers. The young master's only wish was that they should regard his house as their home — " a college situated in a purer air than that of the universities," one of his friends calls Great Tew. The guests were not to feel constrained to observe the hours of meals and bedtime; their time was their own, to be employed as they saw fit — they were to come and go freely, to ride out, read, or work, alone or in company. If on a summer day the weather was too fine in gardens or woods, or if anyone had proposed an interesting subject for discussion, the hands of the clock might make the circuit of the dial; nobody asked the time.

Falkland's experiences within the Opposition party drove him over to the King's side. But he understood perfectly well that no one who seeks to defend what is established throws himself into the fight so wholeheartedly — at least not until the cause is half-lost — as the men who hate an existing reality and fight for something which as yet only exists as the imagination of their own minds. When this image begins to be transferred to the sphere of reality, it is *their* turn to be divided, as their minds become affected by disappointment at the imperfection of all things that are realized here on earth.

The Civil War broke out. Lord Falkland hated the war with his whole sensitive, contemplative soul. The horrors of the battlefields revolted him, and he suffered from the sufferings of his country and countrymen. Nor had he even any great hope that peace could *now* have any good result. Prince Rupert had many of the qualities of a capable general. And there was no lack of personal bravery, loyalty, and fighting spirit in the army. But this could not make amends for the Royalist party's want of money, nor for the superfluity of self-appointed advisers and the uncertainty of the King's policy.

It is related that when King Charles lay in Oxford in the summer of 1643, he and Lord Falkland tried to probe into the future by what was called at that time the *sortes Virgilianæ.* As the faithful in the Middle Ages had sought oracular answers from God by opening the Bible at random, so did the cultured humanists of this age seek their oracles in Virgil. The King opened the *Æneid,* and the passage on which his glance fell read as follows:

Yet let a race untamed and haughty foes
His peaceful entrance with dire arms oppose:
Oppressed with numbers in th'unequal field,
His men discouraged, and himself expell'd,
Let him for succour sue from place to place,

Torn from his subjects, and his son's embrace.
First, let him see his friends in battle slain,
And their untimely fate lament in vain;
And when at length the cruel war shall cease,
On hard conditions may he buy his peace;
Nor let him then enjoy supreme command,
But fall untimely by some hostile hand,
And lie unburied on the barren sand.

Falkland found two lines:

Oh Pallas! thou hast failed thy plighted word,
To fight with caution, not to tempt the sword!

The two men left the library, greatly perturbed. We may suppose that the oracle had merely versed their own forebodings of what the future had in store.

In September of the same year the first Battle of Newbury took place. For the first time Prince Rupert's cavalry were put to flight. Falkland fought with frenzied bravery in the rearguard which was trying to delay the advance of Essex on the road to London. As he charged with his troop across a field which was separated from the road by high hedges, the Royalist cavalry were fired upon from a gap in the hedge. Lord Falkland fell. He was only thirty-three years old.

He is not the least tragic figure among the many who were drawn into the tragedy of the Stuarts. " That little person and small stature was found to contain a great heart, a courage so keen, and a nature so fearless, that no composition of the strongest limbs, and most har-

monious and proportioned presence and strength, ever
more disposed any man to the greatest enterprise,"
writes one of his friends. It is only as an exception, a
kind of interlude between the bloody and tumultuous
periods of history, that the times permit of men of Lord
Falkland's stamp displaying their qualities in peace and
extending their influence beyond a small circle. His bitter words that those who hate the bishops hate them
worse than the Devil, but those who love them do not
really love them so well as their dinner, apply in all
ages. It is indeed true that he who would defend what
is established cannot possibly love it quite uncritically
or desire to preserve it entirely unchanged; that is, unless he is a complete blockhead. Everything that *is*, here
in this world and of this world, is faulty, and he who
loves existing things because they are realities must at
the same time wish to make them better, less imperfect.
And thus he is made to fight on two fronts — to change
that which he would at the same time preserve. He cannot possibly be inspired by the one-sided fanaticism
which is the strength of all who are impelled by hatred
of actual, established things, while reserving their love
for dreams of the future — which anyone can dream
according to his own ideas of perfection. But it is also
true that he who loves some of the good things which
are also realized at all times in the world of things as
they are is tied and restrained when it comes to making
common cause with others. All love has an individual-
istic bias — it can never be the case that two persons

love precisely the same thing in the same way. And all earthly love restricts one's liberty. Hatred on the other hand is a far more uniform and rallying emotion — every demagogue and dictator knows, consciously or unconsciously, that nothing is so useful as hatred for kneading people into a mass under his hands. Then the forces which suck the separate individuals into a mass movement are not felt to be destructive of liberty. To most people it is an intoxicating experience to let one's own ego become absorbed in a group soul or a mass soul.

All the talk about love being stronger than hate, and about good always triumphing over evil in the end and so on, is sheer nonsense — when it is a question of natural love and purely human goodness; although natural human love is a mighty power, and mere pagan goodness has shown itself to be a great and glorious and beautiful thing, an infinite number of times. Nevertheless it has been forced over and over again to yield to evil — fear and hatred and revolt against our earthly lot are the things which impel the natural man to his greatest displays of energy. But the evolutionary doctrine of last century — in so far as it regarded evolution as a progressive movement towards something better day by day, and did not reflect that the evolution of a cancerous tumour or a paralysis is also evolution — was unconsciously dominated by a mediæval religious *sentiment,* although it had rejected the dogmas that lay at the base of that sentiment. And in the same way the view which one still comes across occasionally — assurances that love is the strongest power, or that goodness, or truth, or something of the sort, will triumph in the end — has its origin in an illumination of life which is merely the reflection of a sun which has sunk below the horizon of the modern dechristianized world.

Real, pre-Christian pagans were disposed to believe that the world had once been much better to live in than it appeared to their eyes. In the dawn of time there had been a Golden Age, and evolution had proceeded in the direction of an Iron Age, sword-time, wolf-time, Fimbul-winter. Indian legends tell of a primeval time when men and beasts were friends and the gods dwelt on earth and ruled everything for the best for all living creatures. But then the behaviour of men was such that the gods had enough of them and withdrew from them as far as possible.

It was Christianity, as it was preached by the Church in the Middle Ages to the people of Europe, that gave rise to men's conviction that the world's drama is to end in the triumph of Absolute Good. " None is good, save God." God is Love, God is Truth itself — and *that* is the love which is stronger than hate, Truth, whose final triumph men and devils attempt in vain to oppose. And God's triumph is the triumph of all men whose wills have been directed to seeking to do God's will — even if in their lives they have not been able to keep this direction without wavering and swerving and breaking the line.

The history of Christianity during two thousand years bears witness that men have never found it particularly natural and easy to be truthful and good. The forces which cause the will to deviate from the straight road to God are active and never rest. For brevity's sake they have been summed up from of old under three heads: the Devil, the world, and our own flesh. And to the ordinary run of humanity the last is perhaps the worst tempter. And the most dangerous temptations are not due to the active, sudden flames of desire, " the lusts of the flesh," but to the disinclinations of the flesh, its indolence and sluggishness, our tendency to become creatures of habit. It is by no means the commonest case for a man to turn from God because he loves something which he is determined to make his own at all costs. It is far commoner for him to allow himself to be held back by a love which has conquered him. It is as though we were enticed by the clay of which we are made — if only we could sink back into the clay and make ourselves comfortable in this good created world. Rather let God wait for us than that we should wait for our dinner. Fear and danger and loss are the things that keep us awake, so long as we live on a purely natural plane. — It is the kernel of Christianity that God became man and thereby made our human nature one with His divinity, drew up its indolence and sluggishness into union with the incomprehensible power whereby all things were made, rose again in this, when men had killed it. Unless our natural goodness and our natural, unstable love of truth are penetrated by *that* love and *that* truth which are synonyms of the Creator's power, we shall neverthe-less fall victims to one or other of the seven deadly sins. And the seventh and last is the worst — accidia, sloth.

(1936)

LEO WEISMANTEL

 LEO WEISMANTEL himself describes his book *Maria* as the story of the earthly pilgrimage of the Holy Virgin, God's mother, as seen in the visions of pious women, notably Katharina Emmerich. I must confess that the book left me absolutely cold. It reminded me of the worst specimens I had seen of the Beuron school of religious painting — the frescoes of the lower church at Monte Cassino, for example — with their reminiscences of the styles of bygone ages, lifeless figures in pretentious compositions, and an endless elaboration of decorative detail in costumes and background, which no doubt is all intended to give the paintings a kind of liturgical aspect, but results in a repellent aridity. Weismantel has a weakness for pretentious typographical arrangements, with constant new paragraphs for no obvious reason. And he introduces the whole gallery of relatives with which the old apocryphal gospels and a certain type of legendary fiction have provided the Virgin Mary. With all this crowd of great-

aunts, aunts, cousins of both sexes, and other kinsfolk she is simply the most family-ridden young woman who ever grew up in a tribal community. It is a somewhat wearisome procession, and except by those whose nature inclines them to favour certain peculiarly German forms of solemn significance I believe Weismantel's *Maria* will be found " *ungeniessbar.*"

But a book that is really significant is his three-volume novel about the history of the village of Sparbrot from the 1840's to the post-war period. The first volume especially, *Das alte Dorf,* is an exceedingly beautiful and varied picture of life, besides being a regular gold-mine for the folklorist.

Sparbrot is a little village situated on the southern slope of the Rhön mountains, on the Sinn — a tributary of the Main. At the time the story opens, the Rhön was still wooded. It was the old primeval forest of central Germany, oak and beech with stretches of pine here and there — centuries-old trees with an impenetrable undergrowth of saplings and bushes in many places. The little villages, where a poor population of woodcutters, weavers, charcoal-burners, and quarrymen struggled to support life, were mere insignificant clearings in the great forest. They were isolated and off the beaten track, though for more than a thousand years of the German Empire's history the stream of traffic had flowed past on the river down in the main valley, and through the forest on the ridge of the hills ran the ancient Imperial road, whose two most important stations, in the eyes of

the Sparbrot people, were holy Cologne and rich Nürem-
berg. News and rumours from the outer world reached
these backwoodsmen in a fragmentary and distorted
form. With wars and national disorders they had indeed
been brought in contact, and had suffered from them
directly and indirectly. But the firmly rooted folk of
these small communities had clung with amazing tenac-
ity to their own spiritual store and had been slow to
receive and incorporate new material. Beneath a Catholic tradition of more than a thousand years — St. Boni-
face's Fulda is not far away — pagan beliefs and ways of
thought formed as it were a deep subsoil and gave a
peculiar nourishment and colour to the intense religious
life. Ancient superstitions and primitive rites grow up
like suckers and creepers and twine themselves about
the Church in these regions.

The years pass over Sparbrot with a triple chain of
red-letter days. One of these is the ecclesiastical year
from Advent to Advent, marked with festivals like stars
— the Nativity of Our Lord, His bitter Passion and His
Resurrection, the coming of the Holy Ghost. Then the
Church marches on, spreading the gospel in the world,
telling it piece by piece every Sunday and holy day, until
the last Sunday in November, when the gospel deals with
the Last Judgment. Around every festival there has
gathered a vast number of religious observances and
profane amusements. — The second year is that of Nature, which opens with the coming of spring — the
brooks gurgle under the hollow ice, the sap rises in the

trees and the blood grows restless in young bodies. This year has three festivals: Candlemas, Shrovetide, and the slaughtering season in autumn. — The third year hovered over the folk of Sparbrot like a threatening vulture; it was the weavers' year. In tense anxiety the poor Sparbroters sow flax and hemp and till their patches of ground, with prayers to avert crop failure and bring fine weather. The produce is prepared laboriously by time-honoured methods. Year in, year out the weavers sit at their looms, growing old and withered at their toil or succumbing to the weavers' sickness — consumption. Timid and diffident, the young ones set out from Sparbrot to hawk the linen; they have to travel far afield, for the housewives of the neighbouring towns and country will not buy the products of consumptive cabins.

Miserable huts of wattle daubed with clay are clustered together along the narrow village streets, where dogs and pigs attend to the scavenging, and the children play and sing their round dances. Sparbrot is exposed to avalanches and falls of rock from the mountain, and to floods from the Sinn. The little farming that there is follows immemorial rules and customs, but is accompanied by a profusion of pagan and Christian religious rites. The presbytery is almost the poorest house in the place, the church small and dilapidated, but it is the centre of the people's life. Masses and prayers inaugurate all the red-letter days of Sparbrot's threefold year and of every person's private year. As the church is the very soul of the Christmas and Easter solemnities, so does

it co-operate in the Walpurgis festival, which ends with
a ritual dance and the procession of the young people to
the forest with the object of scaring the witches' ride
away from the village. In summer there are pilgrimages
to Vierzehnheiligen, to Fulda, to St. Kilian in Würz-
burg. With swelling silken banners and lighted candles
the crowd goes on its way singing hymns and litanies:
the sick in search of healing, despairing souls seeking remission of sins and peace with God, while young lads and
girls hope to meet one with whom they have a tryst at the
church of pilgrimage — for they believe it will secure a
happy marriage if they are affianced under the protection of a saint. The pilgrimages are holidays, walking
tours, refreshment for soul and body.

Within his many-coloured garland of legends and
folklore Weismantel has inserted a series of portraits of
people from the old village. The witch and the " wise
man," the village herdsman who passes his lonely life
on the hill pastures, his son who marries a gypsy girl, the
pedlar Hafenmichel with his lively, restless disposition
— it is he who comes in contact with the revolution of
1848 and brings home its ideas, as he understands them,
to the remote forest region. And there is the parish
priest, Tertullian Wolf, whose story forms the conclusion of the first volume. He is a poor lad from one of the
neighbouring villages. From the cradle his parents have
destined him to make amends for their sins. Pious persons help him to complete his schooling and enter the
seminary. Before he has yet taken any vows which bind

him to the altar and celibacy he becomes acquainted with the handsome and warm-blooded Franziska from Würz-burg. They fall in love with each other. Tertullian is still free, he is fully entitled to adopt another career and to marry. The only thing is that he knows why all the people who have helped him hitherto, many of them ill able to afford it and accompanying their gifts with fervent prayers, have made this effort. They have striven to give God a priest who should serve the holy sacrifice of the Mass. And they have expected of him that he should one day remember them in his prayers before the altar. Tertullian feels that he has taken upon himself a sacred obligation. And at the same time he is afraid of the judgment of men. Heroism and cowardice, fear of men and love of mankind build up a wall between him and the joys of love here on earth. And the proud Franziska understands — if she would give herself to the man she loves so passionately, she would nevertheless fail to bring him happiness. So she becomes a nun. And as a Sister of Mercy in the hospital of Würzburg she finds use for her courage, her strength, and her good sense. This brings her happiness, but of another kind: God asks so much more of her than a husband would have had use for, and gives her in return a love which exceeds all earthly measure. Tertullian Wolf becomes a priest, and the grace which does not change but perfects nature makes of the weak and strong man a strange peasant-saint, simple and wise, cheerful and tragic, strict and tender.

Das Sterben in den Gassen tells of the irruption of the

new age at Sparbrot. A stranger settles there — he calls himself Dr. Mehrholz. He is a "*missliebig*" who has some scores outstanding with the authorities of various German states on account of his exploits as a roistering student at a little university and as a revolutionary in 1848. And he is an outlaw in his inmost soul, for having brought upon others, even on his sweetheart, misfortunes which he is unable to forget. At Sparbrot he takes up the cudgels against the ignorance and superstition which allow women in childbed to be tortured to death under the hands of wise women, and tuberculosis to kill or cripple children, while the village wise man doctors them and the priest prays for them. — Sparbrot gets its State school. And the high-minded young teacher and his wife fight against superstition and ignorance, against ancient barbarism, against uneconomic and unhealthy methods of work. Mechanical industry comes to Sparbrot — the factory is to set free the weavers who have been sitting crouched over their looms in all the cottages. A road is constructed to connect Sparbrot with the great arteries of traffic.

Few if any of these men, who are so full of goodwill to heal the wounds and remedy the defects of an ancient community, have any idea of the nature of the living body on which they propose to operate. They do not see that this superstition is an excrescence of a faith on which the people have lived and through which they have preserved their sense of human dignity and honour. They are rightly revolted at the cruelty of the villagers when it is directed against Veva for having accepted the maiden's crown of honour in the May Day dance although she has forfeited her right to it. What they do not understand is that behind these excesses there is a morality which is older than either Christianity or any of the more recent forms of paganism: the vital instinct and defensive impulse of a tribal community. Before the month of May was dedicated to Mary who gave birth to the Redeemer of sinners, the maidens' dance in the spring night was part of a cult of tribal divinities who never forgave sins against the tribal laws; when it is a question of ritual acts which can only be performed by virgins we never hear of mercy being shown to the girl who takes part in them without fulfilling all the conditions. — The old country and the old village fare as would a sick body in the hands of physicians who combat the morbid symptoms without being aware that they are killing the patient with their cures. The factory which was to set free the workers of the old cottage-industry merely consigns them to a worse slavery — and when it has to close down owing to a slump, there is worse distress in Sparbrot than before. Excessive felling strips the mountain of its cloak of woods; the new road, instead of opening up new sources of income to the Sparbroters, brings them newcomers who try to exploit them. The old community, where life grew like the trees with their roots deep in the old soil of Germany, reaching out every shoot towards the all-embracing sky, is dead already, when one night the village is burnt down. The priest, Tertullian

Wolf, has put on his vestments and carried out the Sacrament. He stands in the churchyard holding up the monstrance in benediction before the sea of flames, till a blazing beam from the church tower strikes him down.

The herdsman's cabin and that of the pedlar Hafenmichel are all that is left of the old time when the new Sparbrot is built of stone along regularly laid-out streets. At this time Hafenmichel's youngest son, the tailor's apprentice August, goes out into the world. The third volume, *Die Geschichte des Hauses Herkommer,* tells of his adventures. He and his wife, the seamstress, toil and stint themselves till they can start a little shop. August carries on business as a buyer-up, first of fruit from the country round, then of all kinds of agricultural produce. His firm, Herkommer of Sparbrot, becomes known far and wide. Hafenmichel's grandchildren are gentlefolk.

Nevertheless the family's business talent is of a peculiar kind. The Herkommers are impulsive visionaries, with a flair for finding new outlets, full of a craving for self-assertion, since every threat of a set-back and every hint of a slight in reality hits them so hard. It is a fine point, and undoubtedly a true one, to make August Herkommer's younger son, the priest Johannes, the member of the family who in the end shows most sense of realities. It is he who has to try to save what he can from the wreck of his brother Matthæus, the head of the firm; it is to him that Matthæus's young sons turn for advice and support when the house of Herkommer crashes after the World War. Through his education and his work as a priest Johannes Herkommer's brain has been trained to develop a more sober sense of reality than is possessed by those of the family who have been engaged in big business operations and have been finally sucked into the fantastic economy of the war years and the post-war period.

The last part of the trilogy, however, seems to me at any rate to be weaker than the two first. And one asks oneself whether it can really be possible, even in post-war Germany, that not merely an individual speculator or not too honest banker, but practically all the business men and officials with whom Matthæus Herkommer has to deal, continue to trade with him and treat him as a responsible person long after his insanity is established and can be referred to a physical malady, renal atrophy.

The whole trilogy, however, is a broadly designed and unusually significant work, which helps one to comprehend much of what has happened in Germany since the war and is happening there today. There is power and great beauty in the descriptions of the old German " Volkheit," whose values were destroyed by people who desired its renewal and recovery from ancient ills and defects. Leo Weismantel's cycle of novels about Spar-brot, Das alte Dorf, is so rich and valuable a work that all who wish to be acquainted with recent German literature must be advised not on any account to overlook it.

(1934)

SUMMER IN GOTLAND

 WE always know beforehand what newspaper men will ask a visitor. What impressed me most of all the things I had seen in Gotland? Gotland.

Well, Visby is wonderful. Of course we have all seen the most enticing views of that town over and over again — posters in railway waiting-rooms showing idyllic bits of streets that wind charmingly between low houses and garden walls surmounted by old trees, and churches in ruins. St. Karin's clusters of slender Gothic columns and pointed arches against a blue sky, St. Drotten's and St. Lars's pompous Romanesque masses, St. Olof's gable with the rose window and ancient ivy clinging to the ruin. The unbroken line of the town wall with its frowning range of watch-towers — there was a picture of this in the geography we used in my schooldays, more than forty years ago. Almost as far back as I can remember, I have thought I must go to Visby some day. And yet it was no disappointment to see it. It was finer, indeed much finer, than I had imagined it in advance.

The island is about seventy-five miles long and thirty miles across at its broadest, and it has ninety-one stone churches of the Middle Ages scattered over its surface. All are of historical and artistic interest. Some are real architectural pearls, some treasuries of sculpture — in stone from the Romanesque and in wood from the Gothic period. In many of them there are remains of excellent stained glass — there were workshops for this in Visby — in others there are wall-paintings. And all of them are so perfectly fitted into the landscape that it is a sight to see them: Tingstäde Church on the hill above the marsh, Östergarn's underneath the limestone cliff, Fröiel's Church standing high with a view over the sea and the Karls Islands, Etelhem's among groves in which the ground was white as foam with flowering broad-leaved garlic, Roma and Rone in charming villages. Each new church I came to was a happy adventure — quite unexpected, for I did not know much about them beforehand.

Four or five of the country churches are in ruins. That of Ardre lies close to the main road, but on a lower level. Half buried in brushwood and sunk in a lush meadow, the old walls are bright with the limestone peculiar to the island. I reached the abandoned Church of Bara one evening as the last gold of the sunset glowed in the clouds above the wood. The ruin shone with a ghostly pallor against the meadow, which was already darkening in the twilight, and the tops of the firs were black against the sky. It was too late to go up Bara hill, where in heathen times there was a place of sacrifice by a sacred yew tree, and too late to search for the holy well. But the air tasted and smelt like cold spring water, spiced with the cold nocturnal scents of the woods.

And it was on a forenoon that I arrived at the deserted Church of Gans. This too stands in a meadow among the woods, and the sun was shining on the bright old walls. The grass, where the graves lay levelled with the surface, was full of buttercups and the glorious purple orchis which they call *ormnyckla* (bunch of snakes) in Gotland. Around the old churchyard the wood was drenched with sunshine; above the tree-tops white summer clouds welled up in the blue sky. There is another holy well by Gans Church. Under some trees on the edge of a field the limestone rock is exposed, and in a crevice of this the water bubbles up, icy cold and transparently black like dark glass.

In all the years when I did not know what to believe in and therefore preferred to leave all beliefs alone, whenever I came to a place where living water welled up, blessedly cold and sweet and pure, from the earth's dark bosom, I felt that after all it must be wrong not to believe in anything. For to dip one's hot hands in one of the earth's throbbing veins, to wash away dust and perspiration and to drink the cold spring water, and then go off without a word of thanks, one does feel this in the very marrow of one's soul to be a rude and churlish act.

It seems to me that the cult of springs is a religious practice which normal human beings must feel called upon
to perform, unless they make an effort to restrain themselves. I remember, on a walking tour when I was about
twenty, we came to the spring by Vatnaas chapel in the
forest between Sigdal and Numedal. Thick blue-black
thunder-clouds with glowing red edges were climbing
up behind a wall of dark pine-woods; the water in the
pool round the spring looked deep and dark, and we
knelt down and drank it, three girls who believed in
nothing definite, but we dropped silver coins into the
hole from which the water welled up, to " whatever gods
there be."

It has been one of the current accusations against the
first Christian missionaries in Scandinavia — and everywhere else for that matter — that they brutally suppressed the ancient national religions and allowed the
peoples to keep their ancient national paganism in peace,
with just a lick of Christian colour on the outside. These
imputations are not such absolute nonsense as they may
seem to be when one first meets with their apparent
self-contradiction. It is true that the Church exerted all
her energy in exterminating paganism, without much
respect for archæological and folklorist considerations,
or for characteristic racial values, which were swept
away with the rest when zealous missionaries destroyed
heathen temples, cut down the sacred trees on which the
heathen had hung victims to Odin, the hanged Ás, and

overturned the sacrificial stones on which the priests of former days had broken the backbones of thralls and prisoners. But it is also true that the Church openly and without false modesty gave her blessing to the ancient popular feasts of solstice and equinox. The festival commemorating the birth of Jesus in an outhouse took the place of the ancient festivals at the winter solstice. And the fire festival at midsummer which shines like a star, as the year begins to decline towards autumn and darkness, was given to the forerunner who had said of Jesus and himself, as he set out on his journey down into the valley of the shadow of death: " He must increase, but I must decrease." The ancient festivals of seedtime and harvest and all kinds of husbandry were placed under a celestial agricultural council of saints and continued, purified of their rankest pagan features and consecrated by Christian services and prayers. And the Church raised crosses and chapels and churches at the ancient holy wells, as one readdresses a letter. For it was as clear as spring water that no one ought ever to pass a spring without drinking of its water and thanking God for one of the best things He has created on earth.

I drank of the holy wells at the deserted Church of Gans and at Bro Church. At Bro it is the custom even today to make an offering to the church, so this was very convenient — I only had to put my money in the poor-box. So I thought — but afterwards I discovered that I ought to have put it through the keyhole, or slid it in under the church door. I hope it made no difference. Though probably the offerings through the keyhole were really intended for candles and the like.

But everything you see there — sights, glories, tourist attractions, or whatever one may please to call it — is *on* Gotland, most emphatically. For the island is as flat as a table, laden with all its good things. Or more correctly, the surface is slightly convex, like a shield, and tilted a little. On the west the island rises out of the Baltic with perpendicular limestone cliffs which the sea has undermined, forming overhanging ledges and caves, and off the coast curiously turned pillars of harder rock have been left standing; *raukar* they are called locally. But above the cliffs the island is quite flat, as flat as a pancake it appears to Norwegian eyes, and very gently, almost imperceptibly, its stone shield slopes down towards the south-east, where in many places the land runs out into the Baltic with woods and flowery meadows and sandy beaches lapped by the waves.

On Gotland the primitive rock lies far below sea-level, and what projects is stratum upon stratum of sedimentary rocks. In geological periods when what is now known by the geographical designation of Scandinavia lay deeper in the sea than at present; stratum after stratum of calcareous mud, sand, and clay on the sea-bottom was transformed into rock, sandstone, marly limestone, and limestone. And the new land rose above sea-level, the ice-sheet covered it and has left behind on Gotland gravel and boulders from the basic rock far in the interior of Sweden; the sea rose again, and the old beaches are visible as banks of shingle, one inside the other on the island.

In close proximity to the ancient beaches are found the earliest traces of human habitation on the island — the fisherfolk and hunters of the Bone and Old Stone Age. They had to retreat before the sea to higher ground. They followed the small watercourses which ran out on to the beach from shallow tarns and lakes in the interior of the island, and thus they penetrated inland and settled on the edge of the great forest which there covered the surface. — How is it that the tradition of this flight before the sea has been able to survive from the days of these primitive hunters and has been told from generation to generation for six thousand years or so, until the latest legendary account of it was written down some time in the fourteenth century after Christ? — The Guter Saga tells of the first man who found Gotland; his name was Tjelvar. At that time Gotland had a way of sinking below the sea in the daytime, but the island came up at night. But Tjelvar first brought fire into the country, and after that it never sank again. Tjelvar's son was called Havde and had a wife called White Star. They dwelt on the island, and from their sons, Gute and Grajper and Gunfiaun, the Gotlanders are descended.

In the month of June, when the orchards surrounding the farms are in blossom, and wild fruit-trees, crab-apple, bird-cherry, and sloe, bloom on the edge of the woods, along the roads, and in the meadows — when all the glades of the pine forest are blue with great wood-violets and the pasque-flower has shed its blossom on all dry ground, so that its long-haired seed-capsules shine like little silver tassels — in the light June nights when the air is filled with the brilliance and coolness of the sea, then one can well imagine the myth to be true. Even if some of us might be too pedantic to recognize her among the sooty skin-clad women of the settlement, supposing we could have a vision of the first dwellers on the beach between sea and forest, nevertheless it is perfectly certain that she who first made her home here was called White Star.

2

As early as the New Stone Age — that is, from about the middle of the third millennium B.C. — White Star's descendants had spread over the island. Graves and finds of votive offerings — collections of stone weapons set out in such a way as to show that they were offered to the powers controlling life and fate — are memories of the earliest Gotland peasants. From that time on there is abundance of relics of the people who lived here for thousands of years. They bear witness that the " Guter " found it a good land to live in, good to die in. " The Pearl of the Baltic " Gotland is called in tourist advertisements. Though the name is modern, and rather detestable, it expresses a feeling which is very ancient. The

local forts, the Torsburg, the coast defences in Tingstäde marsh, the town walls of Visby, tell of the Gotlanders' determination to defend their island and to
hold on to the rocky land of their forefathers. The
house-sites, the graves, the churches tell the same story:
of a love of home which was immemorial when the people of the island were converted to Christianity, and
which was Christianized together with the Gotlanders.

The huge burial cairns date from the Bronze Age.
Thousands of wagon-loads of boulders from the beach
were heaped up over the bones of men and women of
the ruling families. One of these cairns, " Bro stainkalm," stands on the bare rock within a pine-wood,
where the limestone crops out in huge flat slabs, worn
smooth and scored by the glaciers of the Ice Age. Nothing grows on these naked ledges except a little lichen and
tufts of hare's-foot, which I have never seen flowering so
abundantly as here nor in so many shades of colour —
from white and ivory yellow to pink and salmon and
purple. There is a hot, acrid scent of pine and dried-up
moss from the scattered copse surrounding the rock on
which the cairn is situated. At the edge of the wood on
the other side of the road stand two sculptured stones of
the Viking Age, but traditionally known as " Bro aikar "
— oxen. The story goes that a peasant was driving his
child, who was born blind, to the votive Church of Bro
and had promised to give the oxen which drew the cart
to " the holy cross of Bro " if the child recovered his
sight. When they had come as far as Bro stainkalm the

boy cried out: " Father, father, I can see the church! "
But then the man decided to turn back — he was a great
miser and thought he might now save his oxen. They
were then turned to stone, and there they stand. A little
farther east along the road there are two more sculptured
stones, and these are called " Bro stainkäringar," for it
was afterwards said that they were two old women who
were turned to stone for quarrelling on the way to the
Yuletide Mass. With the preaching of the new doctrine
from the old sanctuary the old monuments were reinterpreted. But this spot, by Bro spring, must always have
been very holy. As far as I could see, the stream runs due
north, and water that runs northward has always been
something out of the common.

Otherwise the graves of the Bronze Age are mostly
near the coast. One of the cairns is called " Angantyr's
rör." Anganty and his eleven brothers were the sons of
Arngrim from Bolmey. They were vikings and berserks.
They wooed Ingebjörg, daughter of the King of Uppsal,
and Hjalmar the proud-hearted, whom Ingebjörg loved,
challenged them to "holmgang " — ordeal by battle.
The champions met on an island in the sea — the saga
says, by the way, that it was Samsö. Accompanying
Hjalmar was his foster-brother, Orvar-Odd from Rav-
nista in Namdal. Orvar-Odd killed the eleven sons of
Arngrim with his club, while Hjalmar fought with
Anganty and slew him, but himself received his death-
wound from Tyrving, Anganty's magic sword. Over the
sons of Arngrim a mound was cast up on the heath by

the sea where the fight had taken place. But Orvar-Odd bore Hjalmar's body to Uppsal and laid it down before the door of Ingebjörg's maiden bower. When Ingebjörg came out and saw the dead man — she neither lamented nor wept; she bent over Hjalmar's corpse and sank upon it, dead, for her heart was broken. — Hervor, Anganty's daughter, was a shield-maiden. She went to Samsö to her father's grave in order to recover Tyrving, which had the property of dealing death whenever it was drawn from its sheath. At night Hervor brewed magic on the beach by the grave and uttered enchantments, till the mound burst into flames and her father, the dead man, stood forth in the fire. Against his will he was forced to give up the sword to his daughter, but he foretold that she would see her own son die by it.

The saga is late mediæval, romantic and full of imitations of the old Edda lays — typical of a literary fashion which, far on in the Christian Middle Ages, was devoted to viking romance. As in all sagas of this type the lyrics are the best part. Hjalmar's death song is very beautiful:

> Wounds have I sixteen,
> Torn is my byrnie,
> Darkness comes on me,
> I cannot rise.
> Close to the heart
> Bit Anganty's sword,
> Sharp was its edge
> Tempered in venom.

Draw thou the red ring
From off my hand,
Bring it to Ingebjörg
The maiden young.
She the true-hearted
Surely will sorrow,
Hearing I come not
Home to Uppsal.

The raven sitting
High on the tree
Flies now to eastward,
An eagle follows.
For the last time
I give food to eagles,
Glutting them now
With mine own gore.

Anganty's grave is to be found all over the place on
the islands of the Cattegat and the Baltic. I have been
to see Anganty's grave on Samsö — it lies on the slope
above the narrow neck which connects Nordby hills with
Samsö. It was bad weather when I was there. The sky
was blue-black and the sea dark and flecked with foam,
the breakers thundered on the yellow sands and the sea
spray flew over the heather and the burial mound, where
some sheep and I and the Danish lady doctor with whom
I was on a walking tour huddled together on the lee
side. We ate our sandwiches and I drank beer out of the
bottle and poured a few drops on the grave for the dead

man, while the lady doctor lectured me, screaming against the wind. She was a teetotal, evangelical feminist, and by day and by night, in calm or in tempest, she exerted all her powers to convert me.

On hearing that Anganty was also buried on Gotland I naturally decided to pay him a visit. I have known Anganty and Orvar-Odd and Hjalmar since I was a little girl.

This Anganty grave, then, was another of the great Bronze Age cairns, and when I had climbed up the pile of rounded boulders there was a grand view from it. It is situated on a bay of the east coast, and outside the sea lay calm, glittering in the sunlight. Bright-edged fine-weather clouds sailed across the sky, and around the grave the blackthorn was covered with white blossom. The grass of the meadow was sprinkled with " orm-nyckla " and with *Orchis militaris,* the most splendid of all Northern orchises, not found in Norway.

The grave has been rifled, or perhaps excavated — there was a big hollow like a crater in the centre of the cairn. And all at once the stones on which I stood began to roll, and I rolled with them, right down to the bottom of the hole. I grazed my shins, the glass of my watch got broken, and when I had managed to crawl up out of Anganty's grave I discovered I had lost the little gold cross I was wearing. Poor little cross — was that what had annoyed the pixy of the mound?

But, after all, the finest of Gotland's ancient monuments are the great ship settings. They too are graves of the Bronze Age — the later Bronze Age, last millennium B.C. Usually they contain urns with burnt bones. The site of the grave is fenced round with stones driven into the turf in a continuous line, so as to represent the outline of a ship's deck, with stem and stern marked by taller upright stones and the ribs of the ship marked in the same way. Some of them are as much as eighty paces long, and they frequently lie in line ahead or line abreast, little fleets sailing out from the forest towards the sea with the dead on board. There is a strange and solemn beauty about these death ships with their bulwarks of grey stone and their decks of greensward, as they lie within the fir forest and the summer breeze murmurs in the tree-tops and the sun shines on the red stems and the carpet of wood-violets is spread under the trees and over the whole glade.

The belief that the dead were to be borne in their boats across the sea to the other world must have been prevalent in Scandinavia for some thousands of years in any case — even if other ideas of life after death may have coexisted with it — and perhaps it has been temporarily thrust aside and has reasserted itself. The representations of ships in the rock-carvings, which have been interpreted in so many different ways, may perhaps be concerned with the voyage to the realm of death. The Gotland ship settings, our Norwegian ship burials of the Vestfold kings, the sculptured stones in Gotland of the Viking Age with representations of the sea voyage to Odin's world — all these are memorials of dead chieftains. But there are hundreds of finds which show that ordinary landowning peasants were buried, burnt or unburnt, in their boats, with such weapons as formed part of the man's everyday equipment and with his agricultural implements around him.

We are told in the Balder myth that the Æsir laid the dead god out in his ship, *Ringhorn,* and when Balder's wife Nanna saw this her heart broke with grief. Then her body was laid beside her dead husband, the ship was set on fire and drifted out to sea, wrapt in flames.

But behind these legends — of faithful women who die of a broken heart and share the last couch of their beloved in barrow or on funeral pyre — behind the Volsunga Saga's tales of hardhearted and passionate women, Signy Volsung's daughter, who is married to the slayer of her father and her brothers, brings about his death, but afterwards enters the burning house to die with her husband " as willingly as I have lived with him unwillingly," Brynhild, who has Sigurd Fafnisbane murdered, since she cannot get him while he is alive, but kills herself so as to lie by him on the funeral pyre — behind these tales there lurks a memory of an age when in Scandinavia as elsewhere it was a custom that the widow followed her husband to the grave and a woman was slain at the burial of a young unmarried warrior so that he might take a wife with him into the other life. Horses and dogs and hawks, men and women thralls, were sacrificed and sent to accompany the rich dead. These myths and legends were not written down before Christian

times, and doubtless many of them did not assume the
form in which they have come down to us much earlier
than that — though their motives were of great antiquity
even then. And although the Christian writers do not
suppress the tradition of their heathen ancestors' human
sacrifices, the whole tendency of their accounts of the
heroes of the Migrations and the legendary kings and
famous champions of the Viking Age is directed to ideal-
izing the figures and making them romantic. Foreign
sources, contemporary accounts — which are thus much
older than our early texts — give a very different picture
of the exploits of the vikings and of the Northern merchants and slavedealers — of their cruelty, treachery,
and brutality, whether these sources be western Euro-
pean, Byzantine, or Oriental. It is for that matter an
Arab diplomat, Ibn Fadlān, who gives the most drastic
description of life in a Swedish viking town in Russia
during peace-time. He was there some time in the 920's
and among other things had an opportunity of seeing
how a dead chief was buried in his ship. This man of the
harem culture regarded the barbarians' primitive customs with chilly amazement: how a number of the dead
man's friends take the young woman who is to accompany him as his death bride and have sexual intercourse
with her on behalf of the bridegroom, first in their own
tents and finally in the tent on the ship where the body
is lying. After that a couple of them help the bride's
attendant, " the angel of death " she is called, to strangle
the girl, and finally the ship is set on fire. — It is quite

likely that Ibn Fadlān misunderstood one or two points in what he saw — that the girl's resistance when she was to enter the dead man's tent was not due to terror but signified the bride's ceremonial reluctance to being laid in the bridal bed. But his description gives a lively picture of one of these ship cremations — a savage and solemn funeral rite, with ceremonies which even at that time must have been very ancient, handed down from a dim primeval past and embedded like fossils in the customs with which the contemporary vikings and slave-dealers in their Newtown in Russia celebrated a young man's departure to the land of his bygone ancestors.

The great burial-grounds where generation after generation interred its dead belong to the Iron Age. They are often contiguous to the Bronze Age graves: a district or a family used the same cemetery from time immemorial. Some of the graves from about 300 B.C. to the beginning of our era are very beautiful and elaborate: a small mound is thrown up over the ashes of the dead and round its base a circle of stones is set up, often with one or more concentric circles outside the first one.

In the earliest period of the Christian era the Gotlanders again began to bury their dead unburnt, and both burial customs — inhumation and cremation — persisted side by side till the close of the Iron Age. It appears as though the people who buried their dead unburnt imagined the grave as the dead person's dwelling, and accordingly gave him — or her — the necessary equipment, while those who continued to practise cremation fancied that the soul was liberated and flew away as a spirit when the body had been consumed by fire. But doubtless the two conceptions were to some extent merged in one another, and the idea of the voyage of the dead to a distant land still persisted.

At one place it was a school-teacher who showed me over one of these burial-grounds, now covered by the pine forest. Closely packed, the little, low cairns lay sunk in the moss; heath-berry and scrub grew around them and some of the graves had been burst open by the roots of the great firs. The teacher took a burning interest in the antiquities of his native soil, and he declared he could tell by the look of the graves whether they were those of old or young people. For when an old man died his sorrowing relatives took no more trouble over his burial than was strictly necessary; they collected the first stones they could find and piled them up over him. But if the deceased was a young man it was the widow, " his lady," the teacher said in his polite Swedish, who had to build the cairn over him, and she picked out the finest stones, all of a size, and arranged them carefully with loving hands. — The tree-tops murmured over our heads, the sunlight fell upon the heather, turning it golden, the little graves of lichen-grey stones lay sunk among the trees and suddenly made me think of scars in the ground. A thrush began to sing in a tree close by, and farther away the wood-pigeons cooed. And I was wondering how the teacher could be so sure that all marriages in the Iron Age had been so harmonious.

3

THE PAGAN grave-cult is not merely the expression of affection for the dead. According to the ideas of justice of those times the dead could lay claim to a share of their estate; it was their right to take with them some of their personal belongings into the realm of the dead, and it was their right to be escorted out of this life in a manner suited to their rank. No doubt this feeling that people are not deprived of their rights through death, nor the living released from all obligations to them from the same cause, was to some extent responsible for the same tribes, after they were Christianized, being so generous in appointing Masses for the dead. That the historians of later times have lightly assumed that the Scandinavian peoples must have made these contributions unwillingly and only because the men of the Church worked on their fears and superstitions, is another example of a line of thought which we may find in so many connections. Actually the Catholic Church confirmed much of the pre-Christian pagan way of thinking, because this had already grasped something of the individual's profound connection with his fellow-men, even if in heathen times fellow-men meant only the family, the class, and the tribe, and of the community of the living and the dead. Protestantism was from the first, and without the earliest Protestants themselves suspecting it, in alliance with the individualism of a dechristianized generation. In referring people to their own consciences, without any infallible authority with which the decisions of conscience could be confronted, Protestantism made it far too easy for men, who through original sin are all born with an aptitude for egoism and self-worship, to take the impulses of egoism for the voice of conscience — till it became a sort of tacitly accepted maxim that self is the first consideration. The process which was doomed to end in this way was due in great measure to the reformers' dogma that death separates us from the dead like an iron curtain; it is no use our praying for our dead, and the holy dead cannot help us with their intercessions. It is another matter that men's hearts have never ceased to believe otherwise; in spite of the Protestant dogma there have always been mothers who believed that their dead children looked down on them from the bosom of God the Father, and children who were certain that their mother's love accompanied them even when their mother had passed away.

The fact that the grave-goods bestowed upon the dead in heathen times were often so excessively rich as is proved by finds must be partly due to the relatives' fear of cheating the dead man. If they did so there was a great danger that he might "walk." And they were in terror of ghosts; few people dared to seek intercourse with them, to conjure them up like Hervor, Anganty's daughter, and he who would attempt such a thing had to be deeply skilled in magic. Inscriptions and signs which have been found within the graves, on the under side of the stone slabs which overlay the corpse deep down in the mould, customs and pieces of advice which have been preserved among the people down to our own day, bear witness to the manifold precautions that were taken to get the dead man to lie still where he had been laid with all the honours to which he could lay claim, and not to come paying visits to the living. At the same time the finds certainly contradict the theory, which has sometimes been maintained, that the burial customs were *solely* intended to prevent the dead man's walking, so that his successors might be rid of him: religious symbols, very often indicating some kind of sun-worship, are also found in the graves; inscriptions speak of sorrow and of pride in the dead man's exploits, of eternal affection, common to all humanity — this last is nowhere more plainly and beautifully expressed than in a Norwegian runic inscription from Opedal in Hardanger. On the edge of a stone slab — that is, not a memorial stone — which lay in the earth covering some charcoal and ashes, there was carved as with a knife: " Birging, dwell in peace, my sister, dear to me, Vagg." [1] Professor Magnus Olsen, who has interpreted the inscription thus, regards it as dating from the sixth century after Christ. And even if similar feelings do not again find expression on tombstones until far on in the Christian period, this does not entitle us to conclude that they were not those

---

[1] Other runic scholars read, however: "Burial is this: My dear sister Borga must spare me." That is, Borga has been buried in a proper manner; therefore she ought not to trouble her brother by walking.

of thousands of people in the intervening centuries, when they laid a dear one in the earth.

But fear of the dead has always been powerful, and the Church herself has never succeeded entirely in overcoming it; the purely animal terror of corpses and death, which is also shared by the beasts, crops up spontaneously in times when the first thing asked of a man is that he must not be afraid to lose his life, and in times when belief in the holy fellowship and the bond of love between living and dead is strongest. But those outside Christendom were subject not merely to the terror which takes the senses by surprise when men are suddenly faced by deeds of death, even if their whole training tended to make them meet death fearlessly, and to the Christian's horror at the thought of the souls who have not yet found peace, perhaps will never find it. Men were afraid of the spirits of the dead in general, regardless of what they had felt for the dead when alive; and for millenniums this terror of departed spirits has been one of the most powerful motives in determining the shaping of the various cultures. Only in an age in which people thought less and less of their dead, when once they had put them away, and left it to women and children to visit the churchyard and potter about the graves on a summer evening, could it be said, and believed too, that the belief in the immortality of the soul has arisen from men's desire to have more life than the human span on earth and from their need to console themselves for the privations and adversities of their lives by the hope that something far better awaits them. The idea reflects the transformation of the Christian conception of God into the picture of a " family god " such as Brand speaks of, " with skull-cap and bald head " — " The Lord is a reasonable fellow," as Elias Kræmmer put it. Which implies that one has ceased to celebrate the festivals of martyrs and has exchanged the faith in God's inscrutable mercy for confidence in an easily grasped divine good-nature.

The pagan belief in a life after death is nowhere of such a nature as to lead us to suppose it is due to human desires and longings and hopes. At best a happy life after death is reserved for a few. Pre-Christian mystery religions in the Mediterranean countries taught that individuals by going through a series of ordeals and initiations might secure for themselves felicity hereafter, but the great mass of people could only look forward to the joyless shadowy existence of the underworld. And it was not otherwise with our forefathers. Valhall was not a place to which the common man was admitted. It did not even depend on the man's courage, magnanimity, or prowess whether he was to make his way thither at his death; what mattered above all was whether he was born to command. The belief in fate consisted precisely in this, among other things: Fate, not the man himself, determined his lot in time and eternity. So, if the chief faced his destiny with head erect, without whining in misfortune or showing fear of death, it was perhaps not so remarkable after all; thraldom, Hel's hall and Naaströnd and Nivlheim were also a destiny, and those to whom it was allotted had to make the best of it, even if they were a divine pair like Balder and Nanna, or Brynhild choosing to take with Sigurd the road to Hel.

For that matter it was no doctrine of primitive Christianity either that eternal bliss was open to all men, without their making the least effort to attain it. The Church taught that salvation and the grace of God in Jesus Christ is given to all men, and *here* no difference exists between freeman and thrall or between man and woman. But as a mediæval sermon, explaining the difference between free and acquired grace, tells us in a blunt everyday image: "You can take your horse to the water, but you cannot make him drink." The Church brought the means of grace to all, but they had to be at the pains of receiving them.

It has been said that if Masses for the dead were of any avail, it must imply that the rich, who could afford many Masses for themselves and their connections, would derive advantage from their wealth even after death. But the whole tendency of mediæval thought was that rich people probably *needed* more help in purgatory than the poor. Whatever form human covetousness might take, however many great folks, among them the Church's own servants, might give way to greed of goods and money — everyone knew that such faults were human, but nobody thought it right or made any attempt to twist morality into an excuse for capitalist tendencies. It was left for Puritanism to create a moral system which

made a Christian's amassing of wealth no longer suspect
— since Puritanism glorified both the individual's personal industry and his action in keeping others continually at work, but tried to suppress any form of generosity
which might lead to the encouragement of sinful pleasures in oneself or one's fellow-men. And what pleasures
were not sinful?

At best, where wealth had been honestly acquired or
inherited, property in the Middle Ages was held to be a
loan and was called a loan, and he to whom much had
been entrusted had much to account for. And in fact
in mediæval wills the testator constantly speaks of his
fortune as the loan for the administration of which he
has now to account. And at the worst, in cases of wealth
which has been acquired unjustly or doubtfully — . In
short, it was really considered that in any circumstances
the rich might need more Masses for their souls than
other people. But in all Masses for the repose of souls
there are prayers not only for those mentioned by name,
but also for all souls in purgatory. And in all Masses
there are prayers for all the faithful departed. For all
souls the Church had instituted All Souls' Day. For all
souls the children of pious homes were taught to say a
De profundis after the grace before meat and again after
their evening prayer. And there were always some who
founded Masses for all those souls for whom no relatives
had done this. Often it was the clergy who founded such
Masses from their private fortune. In the Ancient Laws
of Norway, for instance, there is printed a document in

which Bishop Olav of Holar in 1479 founds a daily Mass in perpetuity for all deceased Christians. To this purpose he devotes all the sums he has received in fines during his term of office. Perhaps we still do a little, we present-day Catholics — if nothing else we try in November, the month of the dead, to follow the traditions of the Church and do something for the dead. But I remember that, as I walked among the graves of Gotland and saw the monuments in the museums, I thought to myself: how many of us have reason to be ashamed when we see what our ancestors in heathen times did for their dead!

4

" SOLKLOT " — artificially rounded stones which were laid on or within the graves — labyrinths of stones and scratched or carved signs bear witness that sun-worship played an important part in Gotland in pagan times — as almost everywhere else. Many religious ideas, various in nature and origin, lived side by side and to some extent overlapped, here as in all pagan communities. The belief in the Æsir, the " Northern mythology " which we learned in our schooldays, in so far as it really was a religion and not a later literary adaptation of traditions, was certainly an upper-class religion. To the great mass of the people the gods can scarcely have appeared as the plastic figures we know or think we know from the

Icelandic Edda lays. They must certainly have loomed both larger and vaguer, and together with the belief in the gods there survived other conceptions of older divinities and of supernatural beings which were attached to definite localities and families.

We cannot know in detail what the faith was like which expressed itself in all the solar symbols. We can only guess that the solar cult was very ancient and meant a great deal in the life of the people.

One of the commonest solar symbols was the wheel, and where the solar wheel is represented with spokes, four in number, we get a cross surrounded by a ring. When the North became Christianized, the ancient solar symbol was often adapted, and the ring-cross came into being — a cross usually with a tall shaft and decorated with a circular ring around the point of intersection of the arms of the cross. In Gotland it was formerly a common practice for the farmers to set up one of these crosses in the middle of the yard. The shaft was tall and slender as a mast, so that the cross with its ring was seen over the roofs of the houses. Sometimes it was a crucifix which was thus raised high above the home. And we are told that as late as the beginning of last century it was the custom for the household to say prayers every morning round the yard cross — the children knelt on the inside and the grown-ups stood round, the men holding their hats before their faces. If the children asked for their meals before it was time, their mother told them to go out and say a prayer before the cross first, then they should have something to eat. Two or three of these crosses are still standing, but we are told that after the Reformation some at least of the clergy were very eager to have them removed — superstitions were connected with them and the people imagined that fortune would leave the farm if its cross fell and was not set up again.

At many of the farms there was a legend that the first yard cross had been set up by the first owner who had accepted Christianity. He had erected it, not only as a confession of faith, but as a challenge to such of his neighbours as would not hear of any new belief on the island.

The Gotlanders of the Middle Ages asserted that it was St. Olav — Sant Aulä — who converted their island, and they worshipped him as one of their patron saints. Snorre and the Guter Saga agree in the main points when they relate how St. Olav in his flight from Norway in the summer of 1029 lay for a time with his ships off the east coast of the island. The place is now a small wharf attached to a cement works; Slite is its name. On a height on the north side of the bay there still stands an old building which legend claims as the remains of the church St. Olav caused to be built here. In the story the King naturally left its erection to a troll, and on the usual terms: the troll's fee was to be the sun and moon and the King's heart and eyes, unless before the church was finished Olav had guessed the troll's name. And as usual he chanced to hear the troll's wife lulling her child to sleep inside the mountain; she promised it the sun and moon and St. Olav's eyes when Skalle came home. So once more Olav came well out of his whimsical building contract.

Another story of Olav's church-building on Gotland says, however, that some of the local chiefs were already Christians and they visited the Norwegian King on hearing that he was in the harbour. They discussed the progress of the faith in the island and made gifts to each other according to the custom of the time. In conjunction with these Christian chiefs, Ulmer of Månegårds, Ormika of Hejnum, and other leading men, Olav built Akergarn Church on the headland which is still called St. Olofsholm, and drew up, or helped to draw up, the Guters' Christian law.

It may be that the latter story is fairly near the truth. Many of the Gotland seafaring magnates had adopted Christianity abroad, and as early as about the year 1000 there were several Christian churches on the island. But it sounds probable that the Christian Gotlanders should consult with the King when he came to Gotland in this period of conflict between paganism and Christianity. When the fame of his holiness was spread over Scandinavia the Guter claimed their share in him — and Gotland legends associated his name with springs and stones which were supposed to bear marks of his having knelt there in prayer. Most or perhaps all of the churches of Gotland had their image of Olav, so that a number of the finest of his statues that have been preserved from mediæval times come from here.

From nowhere in the North has such a wealth of mediæval art and handicraft been preserved as from Gotland.
I have already mentioned how numerous the churches
are on this little island. Many of them are big enough
for small cathedrals. Several of the smaller village
churches show marks of reconstruction — a small Romanesque nave has been given a huge Gothic choir, and
evidently it was planned to rebuild the whole church by
degrees in a correspondingly handsome style. In many
places stones with reliefs from an older church have been
let into the walls of a newer one. The fame of the Gotland sculptors reached the neighbouring countries, and
fonts from Gotland workshops are to be found both in
Sweden and Denmark and, if I remember rightly, also
in the old Norwegian districts along the coast of the
Skagerrak. There are rich remains of wrought-iron
work, stained glass, fresco paintings, and wood-carving,
both purely decorative objects, church fittings, and statues. As is right and proper the sculptors of White Star's
island represented the Virgin Mary, Star of the Sea, with
special affection and spiritual comprehension. There are
beautiful statues of her as *Sedes Sapientiæ,* the Seat of
Wisdom, with the Child in her lap. But still more beautiful are the statues of her which belonged to groups of
the Crucifixion — with the mother and St. John standing below the cross. Slender and straight as pillars,
growing up out of the noble Gothic folds of the clothing,
stand the sorrowing Mary from Hamra Church, with the
lovely face, full of pain, slightly bent towards the hand

which she has raised to her chin, and the equally beautiful Mary from Öja who presses her hands against her
breast and inclines her delicate little head slightly. The
Gotlanders fashioned these images of strength and still-
ness in sorrow while their island was rich and powerful
and happy, and thus they stood in their churches when
misfortune fell upon Gotland.

That was in the summer of 1361. There was war between Denmark and Sweden, and the Danish King
Valdemar Atterdag had retaken Skåne and Blekinge
from the Swedes in the previous year. It was foreseen
that his next attack would be on Gotland, and the Swedish King had sent word to the Gotlanders bidding them
make ready to receive the enemy. The historical truth
appears to be this: the wealthy, cosmopolitan city of
Visby, where business houses from all the countries of
northern Europe had their branches, was by no means
willing to venture its all in order to continue paying
taxes to King Magnus of Sweden instead of to the King
of Denmark. Visby was laid under heavy contributions
when Valdemar captured the city, but there was no question of such spoliation as is spoken of in later legends.
And on the very next day after his entry Valdemar renewed its privileges and gave the traders of Visby certain
rights in Danish ports. And it does not look as if Visby
lost so very much by coming under Danish rule.

Between half-German Visby and the country districts
of Gotland relations had long been strained and there
had been many conflicts in the course of time. The rich

Gotland landowners had been engaged in shipping and trade with many foreign countries since pagan antiquity. In the Middle Ages they dwelt on their estates in solid stone houses — " castles " posterity has called those of their houses which are still standing, whole or in ruins. But they could not compete with the great merchants of the Hanseatic city; the island's exports of timber and tar, fish and agricultural products came into the hands of the townsfolk and the general prosperity of the country districts declined. But Gotland was still a rich island, and the great landowners were important people in their own localities. And it was chiefly they who rose in arms when Valdemar landed on the west coast in July 1361 and marched north-eastward across the island to attack Visby from the land side.

At Mästerby Church, where the main roads from the four points of the compass intersect, the Danish invaders were met by an army of peasants. But the peasants were inferior in numbers; it was a hopeless fight against an army which consisted in great part of mercenaries — professional soldiers. The Gotlanders fought in vain, and perhaps they were themselves aware of that quite early in the battle. For afterwards a popular legend declared that Valdemar had hired a witch to sit under Ajmunde bridge, over which the peasant army marched, and she conjured the courage and manhood out of the Gotlanders' hearts; that was how they lost the battle.

Near the battlefield of Mästerby stand the first two stone crosses that were raised to commemorate Gotland's disaster. They are great simple stone crosses with a ring round the arms of the cross, and they bear no inscription.

Two days later Valdemar's troops encountered the main body of the peasant army outside the walls of Visby itself. The town was in a posture of defence, the suburbs had been burnt, lest they might afford shelter to the invaders, and doubtless the townsmen had sent reinforcements to the peasant army. On the plain around Solberga nunnery the great slaughter took place. It was said that eighteen hundred Gotlanders fell there. Doubt has been thrown on this figure, as the losses seem excessive compared with what is known of mediæval battles and with the size of the island; but these doubts were dispelled a few years ago when the mass burials around the " Valdemar Cross " were uncovered and examined. The excavations tell us of the desperate fury with which the Gotlanders met the foreign aggressor.

The battle took place on July 27 in the full heat of the summer, and to prevent pestilence being added to the other disasters the bodies of the slain were thrown pell-mell into great pits and covered with slaked lime. Only the uppermost layer of bodies was laid in rows, stretched out side by side. There was no time to strip the dead of their armour: around the grinning skeletons in the museum cling hoods of rusted chain mail and remains of breastplates. The skulls are pierced through by arrows, the jaws smashed, the nasal bones broken, the shin-bones severed at the foot. And the anatomical examination of a number of skeletons shows that the peas-

ant army, judging from these random examples, consisted in approximately one half of its numbers of grown
men capable of bearing arms according to mediæval
ideas. The other half was made up of boys down to the
age of twelve, old men whose toothless jaws had already
coalesced where the teeth had fallen out — one skeleton
is of a hunchback, another of a cripple whose broken
leg was badly joined — and not a few skeletons are of
women who took part in the fight. The peasants had
turned out to a man, they fought like madmen and lost;
warriors and young lads and women and old men and
invalids had all found a common grave under the walls
of the Benedictine convent.

Among these graves the Valdemar Cross was then
raised. It is a tall ring-cross of whitish limestone. The
image of the Crucified is engraved upon it, and the ring
bears an inscription in Latin. It reads in translation:
" In the year of Our Lord 1361, on the third day after
St. James's, the Guter here buried fell by the hands of
the Danes outside the gates of Visby. Pray for them."

Well, the world has seen many wars since that day,
and war has grown worse and more savage from century
to century, according as men have perfected their ma-
chinery of slaughter, and the number of people who have
suffered from the misery of war has risen to six and
seven figures. The destruction of the Gotland army before the walls of Visby was a comparatively small affair,
measured by the standards of our time. Nevertheless —
the bleached skulls which grin at us through their rusted

armour in the show-cases of " Gotland's Fornsal " tell us
in a strangely living way a truth about the nature of war.
Admitting the devilish truth of the statement that the
armaments race among nations increases the danger of
war and that the representatives of the armament industry do the same, these are no more the root cause of war
than the dressmakers of the rue de la Paix were the in-
stigators of the creation of Eve. But both alike are
speculations in a thing which seems to be an inseparable
part of the very nature of man — his capacity for self-
contemplation, or incapacity to desist from it. And
everyone tries to flatter the image he forms of himself;
by tattooing and cosmetics and finery, and by posing it
in proud attitudes. You can always stimulate a warlike
passion in a whole nation by promising that it shall dic-
tate the conditions of existence of another nation. And
the other nation is equally stubborn in its determination
to defend itself to the last, from a rational and intelligi-
ble fear of being made a footstool beneath the triumphant figure of another.

And so it was that the Gotland tradition would not be
content with the idea that its people could be brought
under the foot of the conqueror, except by treachery.
Two separate legendary cycles meet at the " Maiden's
Tower " in the walls of Visby. According to one the
traitor was Nils Goldsmith of Visby. His proud and
beautiful daughter had conceived a hatred of the townsfolk, because she was looked down upon by the rich
councillors and their wives. So father and daughter

made their way to Denmark. Nils Goldsmith incited Valdemar to attack Visby by telling him of the city's immense wealth: " The swine eat out of silver troughs, and the housewives spin upon golden spindles." Nils Goldsmith and his daughter returned to Visby with the Danish army. And when in the course of the autumn Valdemar had sailed away from Gotland, the citizens of Visby broke one night into the goldsmith's house, killed him and dragged his daughter to the Maiden's Tower, walled her up there, and let her starve to death.

The other legend tells that in the winter before his expedition to Gotland Valdemar had come to the island disguised as a beggar in order to spy out the land. He came to Young-Hanse's farm at Öja one evening when there was a feast, and when he had looked upon Young-Hanse's fair daughter awhile the King forgot his disguise and invited her to dance with him. For this the master of the house gave the beggar a box on the ears. But the girl had already looked too deeply into the stranger's eyes. At night she came to him in his chamber; then she discovered that he wore a silken shirt under his rags. And the poor lost child became a traitress to her own people and told her lover all he desired to know.

When Valdemar landed in the following summer, the King and Young-Hanse met on the moor by Mästerby and the Gotlander fell to a shot from the King's cross-bow — that was his thanks for the box on the ears. And one of the stone crosses at Mästerby is said to mark the very spot where Young-Hanse fell. When later in the summer Valdemar's men ravaged the country, Young-Hanse's farm was spared — Valdemar had told the girl to hang out a white cloth and her property would not be molested. But this put the Gotlanders on the track of the traitress. And Valdemar broke his promise and did not take the girl with him when he sailed away in the autumn. So she was seized by her countrymen, confessed all, and suffered death by starvation in the Maiden's Tower.

Now, of course, King Valdemar's movements during the previous winter are known; he held councils at this and that place in Denmark, sealed documents, and so on. But it has been conjectured that there may be some foundation for the legend of Young-Hanse's daughter after all — that the King may really have had spies in the island while he was planning his expedition. And an old Danish author, H. F. Ewald, wrote a novel about King Valdemar's spy and Young-Hanse's daughter. But he made it end in their getting married; she was duly shut up in the Maiden's Tower by her infuriated countrymen, but her Danish husband set her free and together they went to Denmark, where they lived happily ever after — and her father and kinsmen and the friends of her childhood and thousands of her brave countrymen were rotting in the moor at Mästerby and in the common graves at Solberga nunnery. I remember how indignant I was when I read this novel as a child — I made up a sequel of my own, in which the woman who had betrayed her country was finally driven mad by the torments of her conscience, and then there was to come a priest from Gotland — he might be a travelling monk from one of the convents on the island — and he was to tell her that perhaps God might forgive her in the end, but that here on earth there was neither peace nor forgiveness for one who had been guilty of such treachery.

After the year 1361 no more building was done at the country churches of Gotland. The great plans of extensions that were contemplated in some parishes must have been abandoned, and instead of the splendid statues and church fittings of domestic origin, what little was still provided for the churches was mechanical foreign work or clumsy and amateurish local productions. The commonest of these were groups of the Passion and representations of the tomb of Christ with the body lying in it; the expressions of the faces are sad and gloomy, and the fresco paintings in the churches belonging to this period also show a preference for these subjects. Visby continued to flourish, but the countryside must have received a blow from which it took centuries to recover; and then the island's period of greatness was past and Gotland had become a distant province of Sweden.

On the chancel arch of Fide Church, in the south of the island, there is a painting of Christ as the Man of Sorrows, bound to the pillar, scourged and dripping with blood. The execution is quite artless — the figure is badly drawn, the body is speckled at regular intervals with red spots, drops of blood. On a scroll surrounding

the figure are these words: ÆDES SVCCENSE GENS CÆSA
DOLENS RVIT ENSE — " The temple is burnt down, the
people are slain and fall lamenting before the sword."
If we take out those letters which are Roman numerals
— DVCCCDLVI — we shall get the date 1361.

5

IT is impossible to say how " devout " the Gotlanders
were when they raised their beautiful churches and filled
them with precious things and the best productions of
mediæval art. Speculations as to " how deeply " Christianity had penetrated men's souls are vain. The belief
that the living Christ is actually present in the holy Sacrament of the altar when a duly consecrated priest cele-
brates Mass has impelled the faithful to build houses to
receive Him, as grand and beautiful and worthy as it is
in men's power to make them. But it is probable, because it is in accordance with human nature, that vanity,
a desire to compete with the next parish in the decoration of the church, a hope to make up in one quarter for
sins and omissions in another, have been contributing
motives. History bears witness that the Gotlanders were
capable men of business, legend tells us that they were
hard cases, many of them — ugly stories were whispered
of wrecking along the coasts and of shipwrecked men
who reached land only to be murdered and robbed.
There may be some truth at the bottom of all this, and

yet side by side with these men there may have lived great numbers of men and women whose characters were similar to that of Petrus de Dacia, the Dominican from the convent of Visby, whose biography of the stigmatized virgin Kristina of Stumbelen inadvertently reveals the shining purity and loving godliness of his own soul. But if I were to tell of Brother Petrus here, he would have to have a whole article to himself.

I made a round trip in the southern part of Gotland, as far as Hoburgen. This lofty cliff of pink coral-rag forms the southern point of the island. On the sandy beach at the foot of the cliff *Adonis vernalis* was still flowering. Linnæus found it there when he was in Gotland in 1741. It is strange that it has been left in peace here — otherwise it does not grow wild in Scandinavia except on Oland. The wide-open golden-yellow flowers shone brightly in the sun, and the luxuriant, finely divided foliage lay in great cushions on the white sand. The sight was radiantly beautiful — the same that met " the Ruler of Flowers " and his young followers as they strolled along the beach here collecting all the flowers and grasses, seaweed, flotsam, and fossils — adventurers in the realm of a new young science, and men with the delight of their rococo age in the delicate detail of natural objects.

I visited Fide Church and passed Young-Hanse's home. It is now a very well-kept modern farm. It was fairly late in the afternoon when I turned my steps towards Oja Church; for it is surrounded by groves of trees which are full of nightingales and I wished very much to hear them sing, so it was no use getting there too early. As it happened, they did not sing much the evening I was there; perhaps it was because the weather had turned windy and rather bleak.

Oja Church is built of the fine greenish sandstone which is found locally, and it is one of the most stately country churches in Gotland, with handsome porches and a beautiful interior — a nave and aisles in transitional style from Romanesque to Gothic and a great choir of an earlier period. In the arch separating the choir and nave the celebrated Oja Crucifix still hangs in its old place (the Öja Madonna, on the other hand, is now in the museum at Visby and the figure of St. John is lost).

The crucifix is brilliant with colour and gilding — the painting is no doubt fairly recent, but it is not badly done. The cross is surrounded by the ring, and the latter is worked as a garland of Gothic roses and diamonds, as they are called in the art of the goldsmith. It is the ancient solar symbol, the old sign of religious ideas and worship that has come down from a dim antiquity and has here become a wreath of flowers and jewels around the image of the suffering and triumphant Saviour — marvellously beautiful, regal and human. Within the ring, in the two upper segments of the circle, two choirs of worshipping angels press in towards the God-Man on the cross, and in the two lower fields formed by the ring the Fall of Man and the Expulsion from Paradise are pictured. It is the history of the world, and the history of human religions, the questions and the answer — it is the true relation between ancient paganism and the religion of Christ, expressed in an image so clear and comprehensible that it has been given to very few men to set forth the same things in words.

GLASTONBURY

In the year 60 after the birth of Our Lord, Joseph of Arimathæa with twelve disciples set out for Britain to bring the glad tidings to the people of that island. His road lay through Gaul. Six hundred of the Christians of Gaul were so fired with missionary zeal that they offered to accompany him. In the first glow of their enthusiasm they promised to renounce connubial intercourse in order to be able to support him more powerfully with their intercessions. But the mediæval chronicler who tells the story informs us dryly that only one hundred and fifty of them succeeded in keeping this rash vow. With these hundred and fifty hardy souls and his twelve disciples Joseph of Arimathæa sailed to Britain on a shirt. The rest of the company embarked in a ship which King Solomon had once built right marvellously. So it must have been pretty old. But no doubt the weaker vessels thought it anyhow less hazardous to entrust themselves to this ship than to St. Joseph's shirt.

The legend does not say what became of the six hundred. But St. Joseph and the twelve had to undergo many adventures before they finally came before Arviragus, the heathen King of southern Britain.

At that time the sea extended far over the low country on the east of the Bristol Channel. Islands great and small, overgrown with thickets of alder and osier, stood out above the shallow waters. Through the flat marshes which were flooded at high tide placid streams ran towards the sea; under the misty sky floated an expanse of white and yellow water-lilies. The shores, where a crowd of gulls and waders pecked, were thick with rushes and iris, and carpets of marsh-trefoil covered the quagmires. The inhabitants built their villages out in the mud: driving piles down into the soft ground, they fenced in a patch of bog and filled it up with layer upon layer of wattle-work, logs, clay, and stones — thus they formed a settlement inaccessible to strangers and safe for the tribe, who knew all the fords and watercourses among the islands. Their houses were round huts of interlaced branches supported by posts, the walls were daubed with clay, and the roof was thatched with reeds. Sea-moor-sætas these people were called, and after them the country is known to this day as Somerset. Well, this is mediæval etymology, and in those days nobody could know what has now been revealed by excavation and finds of skulls — namely, that the Sea-moor-sætas, whose " lake villages " were buried in the bogs, were Celt-Iberian tribes and that they disappeared from this part of Britain during the pre-Roman Iron Age, or at any rate before coming in contact with the Roman civilization in Britain.

The Celtic peoples believed that after death their souls were carried in boats towards the west and the sunset, to an island far out in the ocean, where was the spring of rejuvenation and the trees bore wild apples. On the chalk downs of Wiltshire the Celts dwelt in fortified camps. When the sun sank into the banked clouds over the island-studded sea in the west they saw through the golden mist the lofty summits of one of these islands. This they called Ynyswytryn, the glass island, and Avalon, the land of apples.

When Arviragus saw that the Jewish pilgrims were good and peaceful people, he bestowed on them twelve hides of land in Ynyswytryn. When at last they had climbed one of its hills and looked down upon their new home, they were all tired, and therefore this height is called Wearyall Hill. Here St. Joseph struck his staff into the ground, and it took root and became a tree, the holy thorn of Glastonbury. It flowered every year at Christmas and Easter.

When St. Joseph took down the body of Jesus from the cross some clots of blood fell into the bosom of his kirtle. He had preserved these clots of blood in two phials of gold and had carried them with him ever since. He now built a church on Ynyswytryn, of wattle, clay, and straw, and on the altar he placed the phials of the precious blood. Then Christ appeared to St. Joseph and bade him dedicate the church to Mary; but at the top of the highest hill, Glastonbury Tor, he was to build a church and dedicate it to the archangel Michael.

St. Joseph and his twelve disciples made themselves huts and lived as hermits on the Isle of Avalon, serving God. When Joseph died he was interred in the Church of Our Lady, and his disciples inscribed his tomb as he had directed them: " *Ad Britannos veni post Christum sepelevi, Docui, Quievi* " (" To the Britons I came after I had buried Christ, I taught, I rest "). As the disciples died they were always succeeded by others, so that for several hundred years there continued to be twelve anchorites living on Avalon and serving God in the little wattle church.

In 410 the last of the Roman troops were withdrawn from Britain. Left to themselves, the Britons and the descendants of the Roman colonists had to resist as best they could the inroads of pirates from Scotland and Ireland, from Flanders and the North Sea coast of Germany. It is fairly certain that the memory of a British leader's brave struggle to save his people and his country lies at the base of the legends of King Arthur and his knights — and South Wales, Cornwall, and Somerset laid claim to be the scene of Arthur's exploits.

In the great battle on Barham Down King Arthur received his death-wound, and then he gave orders that he should be laid in a boat and taken to Avalon. At Pomparlés — Pons Periculosus — he cast his sword into the river, knowing that he should bear it no more. And he expired among the hermits of Avalon and was buried by them.

In 430 Pope Celestine sent God's servant Patricius from Rome to Ireland to preach the gospel to the people there. As a symbol of the mystery of the Trinity St. Patrick was in the habit of showing a leaf of shamrock, which thus became the national emblem of Ireland. After the Church had been firmly established in Ireland and when St. Patrick himself was growing old, he wished to return to his native land, Britain. He came to Glastonbury, and following his advice the twelve anchorites agreed to adopt a kind of monastic rule. They chose St. Patrick as the first Abbot of Glastonbury.

With one of the brethren he climbed the highest summit of the island. Glastonbury Tor is not quite six hundred feet high, but at that time it was overgrown with " impenetrable forest " and the climb is described as very adventurous. At the top St. Patrick and his companion discovered the ruins of St. Michael's Church and had it repaired. St. Patrick obtained from the Pope twelve years' indulgence for all who visited the Church of Our Lady in Glastonbury and St. Michael's Church on the hill. It appears however to be historically certain that Papal indulgences in connection with visits to a church were first granted by Pope Urban II at Angers in 1069. Nor is any Papal confirmation of St. Patrick's indulgence in existence. But this did not trouble the hosts of Irish pilgrims who throughout the years visited St. Patrick's grave at Glastonbury — and at the same time the nunnery at Bekery on a neighbouring island, where according to tradition St. Bridget was the first Abbess. They preferred to be on the safe side, and so they usually made the round trip, home again to the three spots in Ireland which also laid claim to possess St. Patrick's grave. The " credulous " people of the Middle Ages were considerably more alive to the possibility of mistakes and inaccuracies and exaggerations in what the legends told them than, for instance, the average modern newspaper-reader.

The historical kernel to which all the devious paths of the legends point is, however, that from the first dawn of the Middle Ages there was a firm tradition that Glastonbury had been a Christian sanctuary just as long as Christian men had lived in England — that is, ever since the Roman period. And when the country was overrun by heathen pirates who razed to the ground every trace of Christian civilization on the east side of the island and far inland, the sanctuary on Ynyswytryn among the seamoors was spared as by a miracle; perhaps this is the miracle which is reflected in the Arthurian legends. The Anglo-Saxon conquerors were converted by a new mission from Rome, that of St. Augustine; and the new Church in England was given new centres for its life — York, Canterbury, Ely, and many others. It was not long before the Anglo-Saxon people gave to the Church a shining company of saints. But we cannot be surprised that the ousted and oppressed Celts, who had fought for their lives against the invaders and had been forced to take refuge in the hills and bogs of western Britain, were not very ready to accept the fraternal hand of the newly converted Saxons; and it was particularly natural that they should show unwillingness to be dictated to in ecclesiastical questions by these new Christians, whose fault it was that their religious institutions had become somewhat antiquated in isolation and their Christianity tinged with older beliefs. — But when the Anglo-Saxons penetrated as far as Glastonbury they came neither to destroy nor to reform; with reverence they approached the oldest and the holiest of the holy places of England. We are then given the first glimpse of the ancient wattle church in the light of history — Domus Dei and the secret of the Lord it is called in a document of 1088 — for it was in it that Ine, King of the West Saxons, in 704 issued deeds of gift to the monks of Glastonbury: he gave them lands and privileges, vestments and costly vessels. And he caused a stone church to be built around the wattle church, so that it lay like a relic in its shrine. Finally King Ine himself resigned his royal crown and died as a Benedictine monk in Rome. From his time the ancient sanctuary began to grow rich and powerful.

Old descriptions and pictures of the wattle church show that it was built in the same way as the huts of the lake villages in the vicinity, the excavation of one of which is still proceeding. Within a framework of upright posts the walls consist of interlacing twigs and branches and are made weather-tight with clay; the floor is of stamped clay, with slabs of stone here and there, the roof is thatched with reeds. But of course this method of construction was not peculiar to western Britain, or to any definite period; it was known and practised at various times over the greater part of Europe.

King Ine's monastery was plundered and destroyed by Danish vikings, but the church was saved as by a miracle: the Danes who sought to enter it were instantly struck with blindness. The monastery was rebuilt, and learned men from Ireland were teaching in its school on that notable day in the history of England when a Saxon magnate from Baltonsborough, in the vicinity, brought his son there. The boy was to learn Latin, arithmetic, music, and all such arts and sciences as might be useful to him in his future career at the court of his kinsman King Athelstane. The boy's name was Dunstan.

He himself felt a call to the monastic life, but, as we see, this was not in accordance with the plans of his parents. Nor did it accord with the Devil's plans that a young genius should devote himself to the service of God. So he proceeded to tempt Dunstan to sin. At this time Dunstan had applied himself to the art of the goldsmith; he was in the workshop engaged on a splendid chalice when the Devil in the form of a lovely woman came and tried to fondle the youth. Dunstan was so lacking in sentiment — and in gallantry — that when the fair one became too enterprising he seized her by the nose with a pair of red-hot tongs. The Father of Lies abandoned his incognito and fled, amid frightful howls and an abominable stench of sulphur.

Now, it so happened that at the court of King Athel-stane Dunstan's associates thought he was far too clever and full of knowledge — their own faults probably lay in other directions. They accused him of sorcery, and Dunstan was sent home. He was quite young, he fell in love and had thoughts of marriage; but then the call to the religious life returned stronger than before. He became a Benedictine monk and was ordained priest. And in 945 he was elected Abbot of Glastonbury. He reintroduced the rule of St. Benedict, which had fallen more or less into oblivion, and on inheriting great wealth from his father he used it all in promoting monastic life in England. He established schools of learning in the nunneries as well as the monasteries and exerted himself to provide better education for the priests. And with all this he found time to busy himself with his hobbies, art and handicraft. He built with his own hands an organ at Glastonbury, the fame of which spread far beyond the confines of England.

It is fairly certain that the priests whom Haakon Adalsteinsfostre brought over from England when he made his attempt to Christianize Norway were Benedictines from Glastonbury. The " bonders " burned the churches which King Haakon built in Möre and killed the priests, and not even their names are known here on earth. But it is certain that they did not die in vain, and thus Norway too has received her gifts from wealthy Glastonbury.

Athelstane's half-brother Edmund became King at the

age of twenty-two, and he recalled Dunstan, who was of the same age, to the palace. Under three kings — Edmund, Eadred, and Edgar — St. Dunstan stood beside the throne as a sort of prime minister, and the priest was the soul of the work which had been begun by Alfred and Athelstane and which was now completed. England was united, viking raids were repulsed, the descendants of vikings who had settled in the country were Anglicized, law and order were re-established, and the position of the Church was strengthened so that it could set about its social tasks. And a new harvest of saints proved that it was equal to its real task, the sanctification of men, to which all its other tasks ought merely to lead up. Not all the disasters which afterwards befell England — from the Battle of Maldon to that of Hastings — could undo this work. The superstructure was razed, but the foundation had been firmly laid.

Canute the Great came to Glastonbury to pray at the tomb of his " brother " Edmund Ironside — it was said, rightly or wrongly, that Edmund had been murdered and that Canute at least had not been sorry for it. King Canute increased the wealth of the Abbey with gifts of land. William the Conqueror deposed the last Anglo-Saxon Abbot and forced a Norman Abbot from Caen upon the monks. His rule was so tyrannical that in the end the monks openly rebelled against him and he was suspended for a time. But he returned to Glastonbury, and then began a period of magnificent rebuilding and new building under a line of Norman abbots. But the

ancient wattle church still stood, until the Abbey buildings were burnt down in 1184.

The new Church of Mary was erected in record time,
and its ruins show that it was a jewel of Romanesque
architecture, as perfectly beautiful in its proportions as in
its decorative elements.

During the clearing of the site after the fire " King
Arthur's grave " was rediscovered, fifteen feet below the
surface of the ground. The description of the find shows
that the grave was very like certain Danish burials of the
Bronze Age — with unburnt bodies in coffins of hol-
lowed oak trunks surrounded by stones. Here too, as in
the Danish oak-coffin finds, the Queen's tresses were so
well preserved that when the coffin was opened they still
shone golden, but crumbled away on contact with the
air. Yes — for they actually found the body of Queen
Guenever too, though she does not come into the legendary cycle of King Arthur till far on in the Middle
Ages, when the tales of the warrior King and his champions had become the romance of the knights of the
Round Table. Finally it took shape as the *Morte Dar-
thur* — the story of Lancelot, who with the Queen betrayed his King and tried to maintain some kind of bal-
ance between shame and honour by being more loyal to
his King than all other men, in all things else. But because Lancelot, who imagines he can deceive all men by
this device, never for a moment believes that he can
deceive God, he and Guenever are saved at last — but
not before the hero King and the fairest chivalry in

Christendom and the whole of Britain have been destroyed through their treachery.

At the same time as the Arthurian legends were undergoing this development, old Celtic forms of the popular tale of the table which serves itself — in this case the table is a vessel which is always full of food and drink — took shape as the legend of the Holy Grail. The Sangreal is the cup which Christ used at the institution of the Eucharist, and now it is this cup and not the two gold phials with Christ's blood that St. Joseph of Arimathæa is said to have brought with him to Britain. But in the romance of the Grail Joseph does not die at Glastonbury; he departs again to a mysterious castle in a distant land. And the quest of the Sangreal becomes the highest task and the boldest enterprise of chivalry.

It appears that the monks of Glastonbury were themselves inclined to regard the legends of Joseph of Arimathæa in a rather sober light. In 1345 King Edward III gave a certain John Blome permission to dig at Glastonbury for relics of St. Joseph, if it could be done without disturbing the services of the monks. The monks declared, however, that they knew nothing at all for certain about St. Joseph being buried there — it was a pious belief that he had lived at Glastonbury and might perhaps have been interred there — or at Montacute near Yeovil. — We constantly find, by the way, in going back to the original sources, that it was not in the monasteries that the more fantastic legends arose. It was not Church

tradition in Norway that combined St. Olav's death at
Stiklestad with the eclipse of the sun which occurred a
month later in the same region — the accounts of these
two great events became fused in Iceland. The romanc-
ing capacity of individuals and the local patriotism
which insists that all manner of remarkable things must
have taken place at home are some of the sources of the
wildest legends. Thus it may come about that in the
end the legends acquire as it were a right of citizenship
in ecclesiastical tradition — after the ranks of church or
convent have been recruited times without number from
people of the locality, in whose minds the elements of
Christian knowledge and local legends have been inex-
tricably interwoven since the nursery.

Authorities differ as to the result of John Blome's excavations. Most of the chroniclers seem to think he
found nothing, but one writer assures us that he found
the relics and that they were deposited in an alabaster
shrine in the Church of Our Lady. And *now* visitors to
Glastonbury can inspect St. Joseph of Arimathæa's sar-
cophagus in one of the town's two parish churches — St.
John the Baptist's. It is a stone coffin of late mediæval
date, and formerly, when it stood in the churchyard, it
was called in all simplicity the grave of Thomas Allen.
And an Anglican clergyman has written a vastly ingen-
ious opus to prove that the legend tells us too little
rather than too much: he tries to make it seem probable
that not only was Joseph in England, but St. Paul also,

and perhaps Jesus Himself as a boy. So the sport of constructing history out of guesses and combinations of the oddest material did not die out with the monks.

The written history of Glastonbury throughout the Middle Ages is above all a record of continual building on a grand scale. The Abbey school enjoyed the highest reputation, and the scriptorium sent out excellent manuscripts — but we know from Continental sources that the English monks as a body were considered especially " bookish " throughout the Middle Ages. Hospitality was profuse; as many as five hundred guests at a time were entertained at the Abbot's table. A hostel for poorer pilgrims exists to this day, but now of course as a hotel. Great quantities of food and drink were doled out daily to the necessitous. It is not to be supposed that all these monks who lived here through the ages were holy and blameless men, but we never hear of scandals from Glastonbury. The monks are more likely to have erred in being too easy-going, having too many friends in " the world." There is abundance of evidence that they were popular in the country round. People lived well under the rule of the abbots, and the complaints against the new masters who acquired the Abbey's estates after the Reformation are the same here as everywhere else: they extorted far more than people had been accustomed to pay in the time of the monks, and they would never share a mite of their revenues with any but their friends.

When Thomas Cromwell's visitor came to Glastonbury to scent out accusations against the monks (piquant stories preferred!) he had to report that here there was nothing to communicate: " The brethren be so strait kept, they cannot offend, but," he adds encouragingly, " fain they would, if they might, as they confess; and so the fault is not in them." He had nothing but good to say of Abbot Whiting himself — but he asked pardon for it later.

The naïvest trait in a number of modern Christian movements is the frequently expressed belief that if only we Christians lived entirely according to the will of Christ, the whole world would abandon its hatred of Christianity and be converted to Him. No doubt we must strive to live as God would have us — but for God's sake don't let us dream that this will dispose " the world " more favourably towards Christ! Moreover He Himself has called attention to this: " If the world hate you, know ye that it hath hated Me before you. . . . The servant is not greater than his master. If they have persecuted Me, they will also persecute you. If they have kept My word, they will keep yours also." Are not these last words bitter irony, directed against all comfortable this-life-optimistic Christianity? The sins of Christians, in deed, word, and omission, naturally afford splendid excuses for their persecution. But the world's *hatred* is aimed above all at those Christians who live entirely according to their faith. Nor was it any different in the age of the Reformation: a great cry was made about scandals, true and untrue, the reprobation was genuine enough — but it was the saints who were dragged to the place of execution.

Abbot Whiting and his monks had acknowledged Henry VIII as the supreme head of the English Church *in temporalibus* — in worldly matters. And, as we have seen, it was not possible to find any charges against the Abbey which might be suitable for publication. So it is uncertain to this day what pretext was used for arresting the Abbot and carrying him to the Tower. That he refused to acknowledge the King's Papacy in England, that he was in possession of a book which took the Queen's part in the suit between Henry and Catherine — these were only rumours. On the other hand there exist long inventories of the proceeds of plundering the Church and documents showing how the monastic estates passed from hand to hand. For Henry VIII, who had promised that if only he could take the property of the Church and the monasteries, the people would never more be troubled with taxes and economic burdens, let all this wealth trickle through his fingers like dry sand. His favourites and helpers and his changing families-in-law battened on it like vultures.

According to law the Abbot of Glastonbury could only be tried by his peers in the House of Lords. But he was given no trial, either there or anywhere else. It was doubtless intended to bring him before a court at Glastonbury, for among Cromwell's notes there is found the following " Item. The abbot of Glaston to be tried at

Glaston, and also executed there." But when it came to the point, such formalities were dispensed with. Abbot Whiting was brought back to Somerset; some sort of examination took place in the Bishop's Palace at Wells and the sentence of death was announced. But there was no question of anything resembling a legal trial. And on the following day — November 15, 1539 — Abbot Whiting and two of his monks, John Thorne and Roger James, were taken from Wells to Glastonbury along the miry road through the fens. The dictators of our time have no cause to boast of their progress — King Henry had gone as far as any of them.

On reaching the boundary of Glastonbury the three monks were tied to hurdles and dragged through the mud up to the top of the Tor. By St. Michael's Church, which had been built by saints of old, St. Richard Whiting was hanged like a thief, cut down while still living, ripped open, and so on. A private letter informs Cromwell that he was executed alone, lest he might derive any assistance or encouragement from his spiritual sons — they were executed later in the day. But Richard Whiting prayed for his murderers and " took his death very patiently."

The body was quartered and the quarters exposed at different places in Somerset. The head was impaled over the gate of the Abbey. The Abbey was deserted and plundered; everything of value had been taken away, even to the lead of the roofs. But the Abbey received a saint's head in its place.

The monastery buildings became ruinous. And when

the walls began to collapse, people were allowed to use them as a quarry. They fetched stone for houses and cattle-sheds and for repairing the parish churches, on the maintenance of which the new owners were unwilling to spend money. We have heard this story before — at Hamar Cathedral, for instance. When once leave had been given to utilize the Abbey ruins in this manner, the people hastened their demolition, finally with the help of explosives. And in Oliver Cromwell's time a Puritan soldier, Bates by name, made a pilgrimage to Wearyall Hill and cut down the holy thorn. He chanced to cut off his foot in doing so. And shoots — or suckers — of the tree were preserved. So now there are " holy thorns " in many of the town's gardens. It is a species of white hawthorn, more slender and with smaller blooms than the ordinary, and it has no thorns. It usually flowers a second time in late autumn or early winter. And botanists are unable to agree as to where the species came from.

I had my first sight of Glastonbury Tor from the train, which runs in a great curve round the hill. As it rears itself, green and bare of trees, with its tower pointing like a grey finger towards the summer sky, it appears much higher than it really is, as the country round is so flat. On the old sea-bottom the meadows were bright with daisies and buttercups, the fields were intersected by drains which reflected the blue sky and bright fine-weather clouds, and everywhere red cows and grey sheep with young white lambs were grazing.

The situation of Glastonbury, under the sides of three hills, is nice and picturesque — to use two favourite English adjectives — with grey houses and warm reddish-brown roofs overshadowed by fine big trees. It now has four thousand inhabitants. Many of the houses are so old that no one knows their age. In repairing them people constantly come across a mediæval fireplace or fine oak beams, vaulted cellars, and built-up stairs within the thick walls. When I was there they had just discovered many such features in making alterations to a shop which had gone bankrupt. An enterprising lady had bought the house and was turning it into a tea-room, with mediæval chimney-corners and Shakespeare's flowers in the garden. " In the yeare nineteen hundred-and-so-much thys olde hous was maked moch oldere," she might have put up over the doorway.

I had made up my mind that when I came to Glastonbury I would first of all go up the Tor. But first of all, of course, I went to look for a hotel and had tea. After that, however, I did take the path that led to the place of pilgrimage. At first it ran between garden walls, where there was a scent of lilac and wallflower in the warm afternoon sun; then it began to ascend between hedges of blossoming white hawthorn. I came to a sort of fence, and before me was the green conical mass of the hill, nothing but grass, with here and there a clump of golden broom. And scattered all over the hill were cows and bullocks. And scattered all over the hill were cows and bullocks.

Strictly speaking, they were not much more than

calves, but some of them were pretty nearly full grown. And I don't like cows, unless I am personally acquainted with them. So I sat on the stile and meditated awhile. But when one is on a pilgrimage, as it were, to the place of a martyr's death, one feels ashamed to turn back just because of a few heifers and steers. So I snapped off a switch and went forward. Some of the herd at once drew near to have a look at me. I called to them in Norwegian, with assumed cordiality. But when I put out my hand to scratch the forehead of one of them, it tossed its head to one side; the next one did the same, and with that they all trotted off, making for another fence. And I was not sorry.

The view from the top was sufficient reward. Below me the country lay stretched out for miles on every side, in the verdure of springtime and traversed by bright little watercourses. The farms lay far apart, hidden in clumps of trees. And framing this bright land of summer were low blue ridges looming in the distance — the Mendip Hills on the north and the rounded chalk downs of Wiltshire to the eastward. The wide vault of heaven was pale blue and full of sunny clouds and the song of larks. From the gardens at the foot of the hill came the sharp note of the thrush, and in the little grove away on Wearyall Hill a cuckoo called.

All that is left of the pilgrimage church is the rectangular tower. There are some curious reliefs on it; one, of a woman milking a cow, is traditionally said to represent St. Bridget.

On my way back I passed the little Catholic chapel. It belongs to a congregation of nuns who have an orphanage and take in all kinds of washing, as their notice announces. I arrived just in time for the evening service.

Early next morning I was awakened by the pealing of church bells. It was Coronation Day. And the air was full of chimes as I went down the street, which was decorated with flags and pennons and the portraits of the King and Queen in windows and on walls, and gilt crowns and ropes of red-white-and-blue tissue paper wherever room could be found for them. I had seen this finery being prepared in all the towns I had been through during the last few weeks, but I liked it best at Glastonbury, because there wasn't quite so much of it — and one would hardly call it pretty in itself. But I too had put on a Seventeenth of May bow (the British colours are the same as ours) and went to Mass and heard the priest intone the *Te Deum* — there was no singing; it was a very poor little chapel.

There were hardly any visitors at the Abbey ruins when I was there — the celebrations were already in full swing — but there had been an Anglican service there while I was at Mass. Not very much is left of the buildings, but *now* great care is taken of the little there is, and the grounds surrounding the ruins are laid out as a park and are very beautiful.

The Abbey's nearest neighbours are some almshouses for old women, built by Abbot Bere, Richard Whiting's predecessor. Each of the houses has a little garden, and the foundation has its own chapel, St. Patrick's. A similar foundation for old men is not so well preserved and no longer serves its original purpose.

The festivities were at their height when I came out from the Abbey ruins. They reminded me quite touchingly of a Seventeenth of May at Lillehammer or some other popular festival. There was no children's procession, strictly speaking, but there was a distribution at the Town Hall of mugs with portraits of the royal couple to all the children of the town (ugly, but well-intentioned mugs!) , and afterwards there were sports for the children on the recreation ground — races, obstacle races, and sack races, and many queer kinds of sport, ending with folk-dancing by girls in costume round a Maypole. The funniest part of it was the mammas — for the whole public seemed to know all the performers and followed the competitions with anything but the legendary British phlegm. Next to me stood a mother who cackled and cackled all the time at her Arthur. Arthur was no doubt too small to take part officially in any of the sports, but he had crawled inside the ropes and was tumbling about the track to his heart's content. He simply ignored his mother's existence.

We had brilliant sunshine all day — the newspapers admitted that it had rained in London and most other places. And in the afternoon there was to be a carnival procession through the town — decorated cars and lorries, decorated bicycles and dressed-up Glastonburghers of all ages on horseback and on foot. But it cannot be said that there were very many participants in any of the troops. The best to my mind was a little thing of five or six years old. On a car where a young woman in a white robe was enthroned with helmet and spear and shield like Britannia on the penny-pieces, surrounded by girls dressed or undressed as the case might be to represent the different countries of the Empire, this little mite stood on a pedestal holding a gilt wreath over the head of Britannia. The child wore spectacles, butterfly wings, and a red velvet body-belt and stood staunchly holding out her wreath. The procession advanced slowly and with dignity through the three main streets of the town and all its side streets; for two hours I was constantly meeting it wherever I went. And the little spectacled cupid stood on her pedestal as dogged and serious as ever — a worthy scion of the famous British bull-dog!

As dusk came on, all the four thousand inhabitants, besides people from the country and the nearest villages, streamed up Wearyall Hill, on foot, in cars, and on bicycles. There were to be fireworks and a bonfire to end up with. And the fireworks were really fine. But when the huge bonfire was lighted the homely, small-town Coronation festival was suddenly converted into a thing of fairy-like and overpowering beauty. The wild red flames lighted up the slope of Wearyall Hill, with all the little black figures climbing up or hurrying down — they swarmed on every path. The glare and the shadows played over the little town at the foot of the hill, and the square towers of its two churches stood out faintly pink

in the light. But all around the country lay in soft darkness, black as pitch. Not a light was to be seen (they are
very thrifty with electric light in England, and the houses
are far apart in this region). As one's eyes grew accustomed to the darkness one could discern patches of mist
floating down below — after the warm day exhalations
were rising from ponds and ditches on the low ground.
The hills, the Tor and Wearyall Hill, had again become
islands in a sea over which they shed the glare of the bea-
con. For a brief evening hour the Isle of Avalon was an
isle once more.

DESIGNER'S NOTE

This book is set in the eleven-point size of Linotype Baskerville "opened up" between lines with three points of blank space. The "running title" at the top is set in small capitals of the body type, and the page number is in Caslon numerals spaced apart. The distances, from the top of the paper to the running title, between this title and the parallelogram of type, between the lines of type, between the type and the page number, and the widths of the margins of paper around the type, are all parts of the design. The manipulation of these details aims to provide a cool, quiet type-page, undisturbed by the "fittings" (page number, etc.) without tricks or eccentricities — *easily read.*

A little sense of the perspective of time belongs to a text of this kind. The ornaments try to provide this feeling. Notice that they are drawn to harmonize with the *texture* of the type page. The binding is ornament, purely — no attempt to suggest any other feeling than Now.

The book was composed, printed, and bound by The Plimpton Press, Norwood, Mass. The typographic scheme is based upon a design by W. A. Dwiggins. The paper was made by S. D. Warren Co., Boston.

Date Due

12

Printed in P. E.I. by ISLAND OFFSET